A LOVE STORY FROM GOD

"The Revealing Story of Hope, Second-Chances, and New Beginnings"

Dr. Rick Yohn

HERITAGE BUILDERS PUBLISHING

RIO VISTA, CALIFORNIA; TROY, ALABAMA; MANAGUA, NICARAGUA

HERITAGE BUILDERS PUBLISHING

A LOVE STORY FROM GOD
"The Revealing Story of Hope, Second-Chances,
and New Beginnings"

Copyright © 2018 by Dr. Rick Yohn

First Edition 2018

Cover Design: Tamara Behun
Editing and Book Design: Nord Compo

Published by Heritage Builders Publishing
Rio Vista, California
Troy, Alabama
Managua, Nicaragua

www.HeritageBuildersPublishing.com
1-800-397-8267
ISBN: 978-1-94260398-6

Printed and Bound in the USA

HERITAGE BUILDERS

ACKNOWLEDGEMENTS

I want to thank the following friends (alphabetical order) and family members for their investment of time in looking over various chapters of this manuscript and providing personal insight for potential changes: **Bill Armstrong**, former President of Colorado Christian University, who believed in me enough to hire me as the Dean of Biblical and Theological Studies at The Colorado Christian University. Through Bill's passion for the Lord and insatiable love of God's Word, he inspired me to develop two Masters Programs for the University and write six courses for the two degrees. This became the motivation to attempt a second writing career; **Don Bammes**, my Starbuck's buddy, who liked the chapters I sent him and encouraged me to continue; **Tamara Behun**, my niece, who has designed the covers for all of my reprinted books as well as the one you hold in your hands; **Mary DuCharme**, our good friend for many years, who came to the manuscript with a good Biblical background and grasp of the English language; **Bob Marquardt**, my friend and classmate through Philadelphia College of Bible and Dallas Theological Seminary. He stood in the theological gap to make certain that I kept within our theological framework and offered excellent advice on what was too much or too little in what I included; **Sherman Smith**, my publisher and friend, who believed in me enough to tell me, "*I'll print any book that you write*"; **Aly Yohn**, my daughter-in-law, who read the first three or four chapters and said, "*Dad, you've got to keep writing. I love it!*";

my soul-mate **Linda,** who was always there to make certain I did not give up and to guarantee that I was following all the proper grammatical rules; and our son, **Steve**, an author and pastor, who is a far better writer than I, and one I wish had co-authored this book with me, but was working on his own manuscript at the time. And the interesting caveat to that story is we both completed our manuscripts the same week.

DEDICATION

....

To Linda

The love of my life and my life-mate of 57 years. Linda is a highly-gifted communicator and teacher herself, who has always put my interests above her own. Without her, I never would have attempted a second writing career, after leaving it behind me for the past thirty years. She provided the encouragement and motivation to finish what I started and invested many hours acting as my "sounding board" and proof-reader for this manuscript.

She is the mother of our two grown sons, Ricky and Steven, who have been God's special gift and blessing to the two of us. Indeed, when I said, *"I do"* in 1960, I certainly married up. Linda is the epitome of the woman King Solomon so graciously honored when he wrote, *"A wife of noble character who can find? She is worth far more than rubies. Her husband has full confidence in her and lacks nothing of value . . . Her children arise and call her blessed; her husband also, and he praises her: Many women do noble things, but you surpass them all."* (Proverbs 31:10,11,28-29)

Contents

WHAT THE WORLD
NEEDS NOW

....

Hope, second chances, and new beginnings are the result of a special type of love. It's not the love scene on the big screen or that of trashy love novels, but it's the type of love for which the Greeks had a special name – AGAPE!

Such love does not keep track of the wrongs done to it. This unique love offers forgiveness to those who don't deserve it. It's a love that is greater than laying down one's life for a friend. And this special love is uncommon in many people because it originates from the very heart of God. And when we reject the God of this love, we fail to experience and express the nature of agape love. Later in this chapter, I will introduce you to this agape love expressed throughout the pages of an ancient text, but first allow me to introduce you to that text. Sometimes we refer to it as "The Holy Scriptures", while at other times we just call it the "Bible".

This ancient document is God's revelation to mankind, but it is more than that alone. Consider first its diversity. This amazing book was written by 40 different authors, many of whom did not know about one another because they lived in different centuries. Some of these writers were kings, while others were fishermen. One was a tax collector, while another was an historian and physician. They ranged from young to very old.

Furthermore, these Scriptures were written on three different continents (Asia, Africa, and Europe), and in three different languages (Hebrew, Aramaic, and Greek) over a period of 1500 years. Though the Bible is composed of 66 separate books, it is one book with one amazing story to tell.

What do I mean by that statement? For all its diversity, there is tremendous unity within this one book. For instance, there is one main theme of redemption (the setting free from bondage). Also, there is one chosen nation throughout the Scriptures known as Israel. And there is one central figure from Genesis to Revelation – a man who claimed to be the very son of God, the Messiah, and the Savior of the world. His name is Jesus Christ. But the greatest feature that emerges out of the pages of Holy Scripture is God's agape love for mankind.

It is true that the Bible is filled with wars and battles, as well as plenty of evidence of man's inhumanity to man. You even can find descriptions of events in the Bible that would earn a PG-13, if not an R, rating. Also, there are laws written for a Jewish clientele that Gentiles do not keep, such as the prohibition against eating pork and shellfish. And there are customs that we may not observe in our Western culture, like greeting one another with a holy kiss. However, a very powerful message emerges from the pages of this amazing book. I am referring to the message of love, God's abundant and sacrificial love for every man, woman, and child on Earth.

You will discover this story from the first chapters of Genesis through the closing chapters of Revelation. God's love story begins when He creates man and woman to have a personal relationship with them, and then moves through the lives of individual characters, such as Seth, Enoch, Methuselah, and Noah. The love story continues as God raises up a nation so that He might show His love to the world at large. And it doesn't end there.

When His people were living as slaves in Egypt, God made Himself known to Moses and told him how much He loved these slaves. He revealed His plan to Moses saying, *"I have indeed seen the misery of my people in Egypt. I have heard them crying out because of their slave drivers, and I am concerned about their suffering. So, I have come down to rescue them from the hand of the Egyptians and to bring them up out of that land into a good and spacious land. . ."* (Exodus 3:7-8).

God's story of His love for the men, women, and children of the world continues into the New Testament through the Gospels which reveal His sending His one and only Son, Jesus Christ, into the world to express His love to His creation – *"For God so loved the world that he gave his one and only Son, that whoever believes in him shall not perish, but have eternal life"* (John 3:16). The love story proceeds through the Book of Acts as God raised up a new people, known as the Church. Through this new entity, He determined to share His love story with the entire world, no matter what religious or nonreligious background from which they come. Therefore, Jesus gave His disciples the commission, *"But you will receive power when the Holy Spirit comes on you; and you will be my witnesses in Jerusalem, and in all Judea and Samaria, and to the ends of the earth"* (Acts 1:8). The idea behind this commission was *"Tell the world how much I love them."*

God continues His story throughout the Epistles (letters) to individuals, various churches, and the public at large. These communiqués even define love for us – *"This is love: not that we loved God, but that he loved us and sent his Son as an atoning sacrifice for our sins"* (1 John 4:10). In fact, God's love for us is the very basis by which we can love others, *"We love because he first loved us"* (1 John 4:19).

And the very last Book of the Bible, that completes God's love story, opens with these words from the Apostle John, *"To him who loves us and has freed us from our sins by his blood, and has made us to be a kingdom and priests to serve his God and Father – to him be glory and power for ever and ever! Amen!"* (Revelation 1:5-6)

The Bible is more than a collection of sixty-six separate writings. It is the world's most amazing book, because it alone is God's message of love to you and to me. But how many people know about and have experienced God's love in their lives?

The World Scene

It's a sad commentary on humanity that a day doesn't pass without each one of us being exposed to daily news filled with anger, hatred, violence, and man's inhumanity to man. Profanity and vulgarity have become the norm through talk-radio, television, and electronic devices. Nation rises against nation. People groups fight other people groups. Voices of bigotry permeate our culture along with intolerance, name calling, and outright prejudice. What's wrong with our world? Why is there so much intolerance of someone's views in the political arena? Why can't we "just get along" with one another?

I believe the song writer had it right when he wrote, *"What the world needs now is love sweet love, that's the only thing there's much too little of"*.[1] We all want to be loved, but for some reason it seems to escape many of us. Could it be that mankind is ignorant

---

1. 1965 popular song by Hal David with music composed by Burt Bacharach

of the love that is being offered day after day through the pages of Holy Scripture?

My answer to that question is a resounding yes. We don't know about God's love because we don't know much about the book that tells us about this love. Many people think about God only in terms of a judge. Or perhaps they see Him as a God who does not want us to enjoy life. But is that the God of the Bible? And is judgment truly the message of the Bible? Not at all!

What do we mean by love?

Before we explore this great love book, let's make certain that we are all on the same page and decide on what we mean by love. Our definition or explanation of love most likely comes from how we experience love. It was Dr. Gary Chapman[1] who introduced us to "The Five Love Languages", which include: (1) words of affirmation; (2) quality time; (3) receiving gifts; (4) acts of service; and (5) physical touch. If God is a God of love and His Word is His expression of love, how does His expression of love compare to Chapman's love languages?

Let's evaluate how God compares or contrasts with these descriptions. We'll begin with the five love languages. Does God express **words of affirmation** to us? Without question He certainly does. His expressions are discovered throughout the Scriptures in such passages as the following, where God reveals His love to Israel, *"Since you are precious and honored in my sight, and because I love you, I will give men in exchange for you, and people in exchange*

---

1. Gary Chapman, *The Five Love Languages: How To Express Heartfelt Commitment To Your Mate*, Northfield Press).

for your life. Do not be afraid, for I am with you; I will bring your children from the east and gather you from the west." (Isaiah 43:4-5)

Now let's look at God's demonstration of love by using **quality time**. He is available to us 24/7. He wants quality time with us, but can have it only when we cooperate with Him. He calls to each of us saying, *"I revealed myself to those who did not ask for me; I was found by those who did not seek me. To a nation that did not call on my name, I said, 'Here am I, here am I'. All day long I have held out my hands to an obstinate people, who walk in ways not good, pursuing their own imaginations. . . ".* (Isaiah 65:1-2) We often tell ourselves, "I don't have time to pray or read the Bible". In response, God tells us, *"I have all the time you need for you. If you are ready to pray, I am ready to hear."* If you want to read my Word, my Spirit is ready to enlighten you as you read."

Next, we come to the love expression of **receiving gifts**. Do we receive any gifts from God? Indeed, He is the ultimate gift-giver. To begin with He has given each one of us the gift of life. For most of us He has given us the gift of reason, the gift of eyesight, the gift of hearing, the gift of being mobile. As time passes several of those gifts begin to dissipate due to the aging process, and we then come to realize what a precious gift each of those abilities truly was. He also pours out specific gifts of ability, that we may call "talents". Some people are born with tremendous musical ability. Others have excellent mechanical skills while others possess technical skills. Some of us can draw, paint, or create works of art from scratch.

Then to those who know God in a personal way, He has also distributed "spiritual gifts", which are special abilities used to serve Him – *"We have different gifts, according to the grace given us. If a man's gift is prophesying, let him use it in proportion to his faith. If it is serving, let him serve; if it is teaching, let him teach;*

if it is encouraging, let him encourage; if it is contributing to the needs of others, let him give generously; if it is leadership, let him govern diligently; if it is showing mercy, let him do it cheerfully" (Romans 12:6-8). And on top of these functioning gifts, the greatest gift of all is His Son, Jesus Christ. God loves us and we can know of His love by taking the time to record the many gifts we possess today because of His love for us.

But what about **acts of service**? In what ways, does God serve us? Think of Jesus' own words when He told His disciples, who were arguing as to who was going to be the greatest in the kingdom, *"Instead, whoever wants to become great among you must be your servant, and whoever wants to be first must be slave of all. For even the Son of Man did not come to be served, but to serve, and to give his life as a ransom for many"* (Mark 10:43-45). He serves us by providing for our needs, protecting us, answering our prayers, guiding us through life, and in many other ways.

And then there is that fifth means of communicating one's love and that is by **physical touch.** At first we might think, *"I've never been physically touched by God"*. Does that mean that He therefore does not love us? Certainly not! God is spirit, so we should not expect that physical touch would be a major expression of God's love for us. However, in a very real sense, God touched all of us in a physical way when He sent His Son into the world. Jesus invested a three-plus year ministry touching people, giving sight to the blind, hearing to the deaf, walking to the invalid, and even life to the dead. He touched men, women, and children physically, emotionally, and spiritually. Jesus was God's physical touch to mankind, and today we all benefit from that touch of love.

Now let's move from the expressions of love to three Greek words for love. They are 1) eros, from which we derive the term "erotic"; (2) philos, from which come the terms philosophy (love of wisdom), philanthropy (love of man), and Philadelphia (love of brother or brotherly love); and (3) agape. How do these terms differ from one another? They move from the lowest form of love to the highest type of love.

Eros – a sensual love, a preoccupation with satisfying one's appetites, often outside of moral or ethical boundaries. Though this word is not used in Scripture, it is demonstrated time and again throughout God's Word. This is often the beginning of a love relationship, and too often it is the end of a love relationship. When the senses are no longer titillated, this type of love begins to search for a new relationship.

I've often talked about this type of love as a **"because of love"**. *"Because you are beautiful/handsome, I love you". "Because you make me feel good, I love you". "Because you say nice things about me I love you".*

Philos – a brotherly type of love. It also speaks about a love for things, or having an affection for something. It could include people, food, clothes, entertainment, and other such attractions. Sometimes it is used of God's love for us. Jesus told His disciples, *"No, the Father himself loves you because you have loved me and have believed that I came from God"* (John 16:27).

I've considered this type of love as an **"If love"**. *"If you continue to love me, I'll continue to love you". "If you continue to be my friend, I'll continue to be your friend". "If you keep your part of the bargain in marriage, I'll keep my part".* But when the "if" is not met, the love dissipates and possibly even disappears.

Agape – This love is a giving, self-sacrificing type of love. It is a love that never stopes loving, no matter what the circumstances. It's the love in the marriage vows, *"for better or worse, for richer or poorer, in sickness and in health"*. I've often pictured this as **"in spite of love"**. *"In spite of the fact that you are not nice to me, I still love you"*. *"In spite of the fact that you hurt me, I love you."* *"In spite of the fact that you are aging and losing some of that physical attractiveness, I love you"*.

This is the type of love that God expresses to us daily. Despite our failures, our rebellion, our neglect to honor Him, God continues to love us. Even though we sin against Him, He continues to love us. In fact, the Apostle Paul reminds us of just how great God's love is when he writes, *"But God demonstrates his own love for us in this: While we were still sinners, Christ died for us"* (Romans 5:8). God has never said, *"Once you clean up your life, I'll love you!"* Nor has He ever stated, *"If you behave yourself, I'll love you. But if you step out of line, I am coming to get you"*. God loves us with a giving and self-sacrificing love, no matter who we are or what we have done.

To observe how this agape love expresses itself in everyday life, the Apostle Paul helps us visualize agape love in action. He writes, *"Love is patient, love is kind. It does not envy, it does not boast, it is not proud. It is not rude, it is not self-seeking, it is not easily angered, it keeps no record of wrongs. Love does not delight in evil but rejoices with the truth. It always protects, always trusts, always hopes, always perseveres. Love never fails."* (1 Corinthians 13:4-8)

Now let's remove the word, "love" from this passage and replace it with either God or Jesus, and discover that God is the very essence of love.

"God (Jesus) is patient, God (Jesus) is kind. God (Jesus) does not envy, God (Jesus) does not boast, God (Jesus) is not proud. God (Jesus) is not rude, God (Jesus) is not self-seeking, God (Jesus) is not easily angered, God (Jesus) keeps no record of wrongs. God (Jesus) does not delight in evil but rejoices with the truth. God (Jesus) always protects, always trusts, always hopes, always perseveres. God (Jesus) never fails."

This next step is far more dangerous, but it is worth the comparison. Take out the name of God or Jesus and replace it with your own name. Yes, it does get embarrassing as you move through the qualities and expressions of love, but it provides a basis upon which we can evaluate our personal love for ourselves, our family and others.

Now that we've understood the meaning(s) of love, we will trace God's Love Story throughout the Bible from Genesis to Revelation. We have already dealt with the diversity of this great book we call the Bible, so it's time to consider the unity that tells about God's love for each one of us.

1

The Big Picture of God's Love Story

Like an exquisite painting with its splashes of color, hues, and textures, God's love story emerges through the pages of Holy Scripture. It begins with a dash of color here and there, but eventually explodes into a masterpiece on the Creator's canvas. Likewise, you will begin with a small taste of this magnificent love and soon you are craving for more. At first, the colorful themes of Scripture appear in a soft focus, but soon the focus sharpens, and the depth of God's love becomes so clear, that the observer's heart is challenged to respond. And what are those themes that reveal the love of God? They include sin, redemption, the nation of Israel, and the Lord Jesus Christ.

One of my favorite places in Israel is Mount Arbel. It is a 750-foot cliff located near the city of Tiberius, overlooking the Sea of Galilee. I love to take groups to the top of that cliff because we can see the entire upper half of the Sea of Galilee below. And from that vantage point I can teach about the ministry of Christ around that body of water and focus on such places as Tabgha. That is where Jesus called His first disciples. As we pan to the right we capture a view of the Mount of Beatitudes, where Jesus gave

His Sermon on the Mount (Matthew 5-7); Capernaum, where the Lord lived for three years; Korazin and Bethsaida, two of the three cities where He proclaimed the kingdom of God. However, before we journey to the details of the Bible, let's ascend to a higher location where we can capture an overview of these sixty-six individual books.

Figure 1 - Photo from Mt. Arbel, by Dr. Rick Yohn

Some people look at the Bible and see nothing but sixty-six books with strange titles. Others approach the Scriptures from a merely historical perspective and recognize that it is a complete history of the Jewish nation. Then there are those who focus on the customs and cultures of the people in Scripture. But what many Bible readers miss is God's love revealed in these united themes throughout the Bible. To avoid missing the mother lode of most problems we experience, we will begin with our first theme, sin.

God's Love Through Sin

When we observe the night sky on a cloudless night, we see God's majesty displayed throughout that night sky. Every evening the moon rises, sometimes as a beautiful full moon and at other times a white sliver in the heavens. And during the day, the sun never fails to rise in the East and set in the West. It's never early and never late.

But imagine this – a time when none of that existed. Try to visualize a time of darkness, emptiness and formlessness. And then suddenly a voice calls out, *"Let there be light,"* and then there was light. . . *Let there be an expanse between the waters to separate water from water . . . Let the water under the sky be gathered to one place, and let dry ground appear. . . Let the land produce vegetation.. etc.".* The result? Light, sun, moon, stars, dry land, vegetation, and animals appeared on what was once formless and empty. However, for the best of all creation, God said, *"Let us make man in our image, in our likeness, and let them rule over the fish of the sea and the birds of the air, over the livestock, over all the earth, and over all the creatures that move along the ground.' So God created man in his own image, in the image of God he created him; male and female he created them"* (Genesis 1:26-27). And when the account closes, God rests with great satisfaction – *"God saw all that he had made, and it was very good"* (Genesis 1:31).

Why didn't God stop His creation with living creatures? Though God saw that all He had done was "good", He knew there was something better. He wanted to create something that was "very good". Something that could respond by its own free will to the love God wanted to shower upon the highest of all creation – mankind.

Like a beautiful relationship celebrated in front of the pastor and among many witnesses, vows are exchanged, and each lover makes the commitment of "I do", and then they are off to their honeymoon. But eventually daily, routine life creeps into this budding relationship, and the honeymoon quickly comes to a screeching halt. What was one day termed "very good" some-what turns into, "how did I get myself into this?" Unexpressed and therefore, unknown expectations are not met. Tempers begin to flare. And in some cases, the marriage begins to unravel.

Something similar happened in God's relationship with His most prized of all creation. The "very good" turned into shame, heartache, separation, and eventual death. The innocent first family disobeyed God's very clear directive and took matters into their own hands. What happened in that Garden in the lives of two individuals, who decided to rebel against God, passed down to us from generation to generation. The Bible calls this issue **SIN**. It begins in the Book of Genesis, carries through all 66 Books of the Bible and ends in the Book of Revelation. This is one of the major reasons why so many do not know nor experience God's love daily.

I recognize that the concept of sin means many things to many people. Most people don't think about sin because they've set their standards for what is right and what is wrong, or they follow the standards that society has set. Many believe that what may be wrong for one person may be considered OK for others.

A few years ago, my wife and I were driving from Parker, CO to Ruskin, FL. We decided to make it a four-day journey. Most of the time we were driving on interstates, with the average speed zones between 70-75 miles per hour. When we arrived in Louisi-ana, my wife found a road on the map that looked like a shortcut but was a two-lane road. She said, *"Let's get off the highway for about twenty miles."* It sounded like a good idea, so, I turned from the highway to the two-lane road.

The road was narrow but straight. On both sides of the narrow road were deep crevices filled with water. In one of them, I saw an alligator swimming in the water. I immediately decided to grip the steering wheel a little tighter. I was making good time at about 72 miles per hour. The only problem was that the speed zone posted 55 miles per hour. Because I thought I was safe at 72 miles per hour, I paid no attention to the posted sign. After all, who else would be crazy enough to be on this road with steep crevices and alligators? And then it happened. A truck coming toward me looked a little suspicious. Suddenly I realized that it was a Louisiana State Patrol. I quickly slowed down, but it was too late! He whipped around and pulled me over. I accepted my penalty and painfully made a large donation to the Louisiana State Patrol. My speeding was a "violation" of the law. The State of Louisiana made a law and posted it. I saw it and ignored it. The price for ignoring the posted law was $250.

God, who created us, knows how we will function best in life. He, therefore, set up guidelines, directives, and rules within which we are to live. When we violate them, it is called sin. Though society and individuals make up their standards by which to live, as I did in Louisiana, each will be judged by God's standard, just as the policeman judged me by the standards of Louisiana. For some reason or other, Louisiana ignored the rules that I made for myself and imposed its rule on me. As much as I wished that the officer would have made an exception for me, he followed the rules of his state and penalized me.

The officer issued the ticket and told me that there were too many accidents on that road and cars sometime end up in one of the ditches on either side of the road, the ditches where I saw the alligator swimming. That got my attention!

Likewise, God's doesn't adjust His standards to ours. He is a holy (morally and ethically pure) God with holy standards while man is sinful and willing to develop flexible standards. God sets standards because He created us and knows what is best. Those standards are given out of love for His creation. His purpose is not to judge and make us pay penalties, but rather to protect us from hurting ourselves and others. However, each generation tends to lower the moral and ethical bar. What was considered wrong by society just a few years ago society celebrates today. And when we live by our flexible standards, we usually hurt ourselves and those whom we love.

God Demonstrated His Love In His Provision For Sin

Something motivated God not to destroy mankind. I believe that motive was His love for man. Despite man's rebellious spirit and desire to keep God out of his life, the Lord continues to pursue each one of us and offers us a way back to Him. This idea or topic is known as "redemption." That word has several meanings because there are some Greek words translated redeem, or redemption.

In Genesis 1–11 we read about men who "walked with God" (Enoch) or "found grace in the eyes of the Lord" (Noah). They were righteous men, and Noah was a preacher of righteousness and was a messenger of redemption. But as time passed, God decided to use a nation to proclaim the terms of redemption, and through that nation, provide a Redeemer for all mankind, one who would pay the price of redemption and set men free from the penalty of sin.

That's where the nation of Israel comes on the scene, beginning with Genesis 12 through the last book of the Old Testament, Malachi. It's a people group that started with one man, who today would be known as an Iraqi, for he came from present day Iraq. His name was Abram, later changed to Abraham, which means, "father of many nations".

God's Demonstrated His Love Through A Nation

Throughout Scripture you'll read about the many nations of the world that existed during the time of Abraham, Moses, David and the Prophets. But those nations are mentioned primarily as they relate to the nation of Israel. They are either at war with Israel, under the dominance of Israel or in the process of making peace with Israel. Israel is known as "The Chosen People." You may wonder why God chose that nation. Was it because the people were so righteous? Or perhaps because they were a huge people group? Or maybe because they were very powerful and possessed weapons that other nations did not have. The answer is none of the above.

Many of the Jews during Moses day had the same question in their minds. Those who thought that they were special, or that they were better or smarter than other nations would have been sorely disappointed when God answered that question for them. Here's His answer to Israel – *"The Lord did not set his affection on you and choose you because you were more numerous than other peoples, for you were the fewest of all peoples. But it was because the Lord loved you and kept the oath he swore to your forefathers that he brought you out with a mighty hand and redeemed you from the land of slavery, from the power of Pharaoh king of Egypt."* (Deuteronomy 7:7-8) God had a love story to share with the world and needed a nation to communicate it through their lifestyle and worship of the One true God. However, to accomplish His purpose, God did not begin with a nation that had already existed. He began from scratch, from one man by the name of Abram.

Who was this Abram? He was no one special. There is nothing in his early life that would have caused God to choose Him. Abram was not a great warrior, leader, or highly educated. He was just an ordinary man whom God decided to select out of a Middle-Eastern country. And when God chose Abram, He promised that He would make him the father of many nations. At the time, Abraham had no children and was 75 years old.

Now, why would God to such great lengths to raise up a nation who would hopefully convey His love through redemption to the world? The only plausible explanation is that God wanted the world to know how He had provided for their sin problem. He wanted the message of redemption to go to the other nations, who had no knowledge of who created the heavens and the earth. Israel was going to be God's chosen vehicle through which the nations (Gentiles) would come to know TRUE love and worship their Creator.

However, Israel failed at that responsibility. They left the God who had showered His love upon them time and again. He redeemed them from Egyptian bondage and redeemed them from their seventy-year exile in Babylon. But Israel continued to follow its own rules and regulations and ignore God's love. So, God raised up another messenger. One who would represent God perfectly. A man who would always remain faithful, and would become the Redeemer of all mankind. This is the man who surrounded Himself with twelve other men to carry His love story to the world after He was gone.

God Demonstrated His Love Through One Man

This man called Jesus entered the world uniquely, through a virgin named Mary. He was following the plan laid out between Himself and His Father before He created all things. During the days of the Old Testament and into the New Testament (the Four Gospels – Matthew, Mark, Luke, and John), the means of redemption was through the shedding of the blood of bulls, goats and lambs. Their lives became the substitute for man's sin. The Bible calls this an "atonement" or a "covering." The blood of those animals covered the sins of the people.

However, once we enter the first century A.D., a new way to deal with this one major problem is inaugurated. No longer will the blood of animals satisfy a Just and Holy God. No longer will God tolerate a mere "covering over" of sin. He wanted sin to be dealt with on a permanent basis. God needed a perfect, unblemished, sinless sacrifice.

As much as I enjoy a good movie or a good TV program, I was always more interested in what goes on behind the scenes of a movie or television program. That opportunity arrived when I was a student in seminary. WFAA-TV in Dallas, TX was looking for a camera man to run the floor cameras on the weekends. I quickly volunteered and soon learned what goes on behind the camera. I discovered that TV can be exciting occasionally, when you meet some well-known personality, but it is also very boring, especially when you are waiting for the crew to set up the lights, the camera angles, the sound system and all the other paraphernalia essential for a good production. Along with the waiting, there is often a lot of profanity as the talent yells at the producers and the producers yell at the talent who sit in front of the camera.

However, we do capture a glimpse of an event that occurred behind the scene of creation. On that occasion, a wonderful conversation took place between our Father in Heaven and His Son, Jesus Christ. Listen carefully as we eavesdrop on a conversation that even the angels did not hear. Jesus is speaking to His Father and says, *"Sacrifice and offering you did not desire, but a body you prepared for me; with burnt offerings and sin offerings you were not pleased. Then I said, 'Here I am – it is written about me in the scroll – I have come to do your will O God.'"* (Hebrews 10:6-7).

Pause a moment with me and meditate on what we've just read. The God of all creation knows that there is only one way to deal with sin and that is by providing a sinless sacrifice who would take upon Himself the sin of the world. When I picture this conversation, I can only think of a father talking with his son, who is preparing to go off into battle. The difference here is this. While most parents, who send their sons and daughters into the armed forces, hope and pray that their son will return safely, our heavenly Father knew for certain that His Son would taste death before He returned to heaven in a resurrected body. Jesus was not forced to become our "Redeemer". He volunteered for the task. He was the only One who would qualify to "take away sin" and not merely "cover over" sin.

The word "redemption" conveys the ideas of substituting, purchasing something and paying a price. Because we were slaves of sin, Jesus went to the marketplace of slavery and substituted his life for our lives. The price He paid was His blood on the cross to set us free from the penalty of sin[1]. And He bought us for Himself, that we might enjoy eternity with Him. This One Major Person can be found throughout Scripture from Genesis to Revelation.

A reporter once asked the brilliant theologian of the twentieth century, by the name of Karl Barth, if he could summarize all the theological volumes that he wrote over the years. He thought for a moment and then replied, *"Jesus loves me this I know, for the Bible tells me so"*.

That Sunday School song probably best sums up the reason why God raised up men to write what is known as Holy Scripture. God wanted to make Himself and His love known to us, so that we could enjoy a meaningful life while on earth, as well as a glorious and purposeful life after our earth's journey has been completed.

---

1. Romans 6:17-23

CHAPTER

2

God's Love in Creation

Seeing The Pieces, But Missing The Whole

I recall growing up attending Sunday School and church every Sunday. It was never a matter of, *"Do you want to go to church this morning"*. It was just what we did on Sunday. I can't tell you anything specific that I'd learned, but I could recall Bible stories about Jonah and the great fish, Joseph and his coat of many colors, Moses leading the people out of Egypt, Joshua fighting the battle of Jericho, Jesus healing the blind man, and Zacchaeus climbing the sycamore tree to see Jesus. But I couldn't tell you where any of the pieces of the Biblical puzzle fit together. There was a Joseph in the Old Testament and a Joseph in the New Testament. There were wise men and there were shepherds, but who were they and where did they belong in the story? Did they all show up at the same time and on the same night at Christmas.? And how does any of this relate to God's love?

In this chapter, we will develop a timeline beginning in the Old Testament, and try to get the right people in the right chronological order. Then we'll move into the New Testament and do the same thing there.

We don't know when God created the heavens and the earth, but we know He did create them. We also know that there are some archaeological projects that have uncovered some ancient ruins and date back around nine thousand years. In fact, it's believed that Jericho, a city in Israel, is about nine to ten thousand years old. And yet the focus in the Old Testament is on the nation of Israel that began with a man named Abraham, and he dates to around 2200 B.C. That's four thousand years ago. And yet, the first eleven chapters of Genesis (the first book of the Bible) go back even further to the time of creation. How do we date that? We don't. However, in our overview of God's love story in the Old Testament, we'll go back to creation and move through the first eleven chapters of the first Book of the Bible – Genesis.

History is "His Story"

The entire Bible can be designated by one word – **HISTORY**. By this I don't mean that the Bible is a mere history book, though it is the most complete ancient text on the history of Israel. When you separate the word into two parts you get **HIS STORY**. The Bible is God's Story about who He is and who we are. It is His Story about Redemption, how He has made it possible for each one of us to experience a personal relationship with Him. It's His Story about how sin entered the world and the price man has paid because of his sin. It's His Story about the past, present and future of planet earth.

But most of all, the Bible is His Story about His love for us and His sacrifice that made it possible for us to enjoy eternity with Him. This wonderful story was inspired by the Holy Spirit, who guided forty writers to accurately communicate it over a period of 1500 years through the means of oral and written communication. He guided men to use tablets of stone, sheets of papyrus, animal skin (parchment), and finally paper. The result of this process is what we hold in our hands today and call "The Bible".

What lies between the pages of the world's most amazing book? How did the ancients put it all together so that you and I could hear the "very words of God" telling us about His love? Let's begin with what we call the Old Testament.

A Love Story From God In The Old Testament

The word translated "Testament" is the term, "Covenant". A covenant is an agreement between two parties. And it's often based on the underlying premise, *"I'll do this if you'll do that"*. However, for our purpose in this chapter, we'll just focus on the "Old Covenant" (Testament).

Whenever I teach, I like to make things as clear as possible and so I often will use an acronym (a set of initials representing a name, object or organization). Teaching the Old Testament is no exception, so here's the acronym. Think in terms of **My BaSKET**. The capital letters are those that we use in our understanding of this Old Testament overview. The small letters just help us complete the acronym.

Though the focus of the Old Testament is the people (nation) of Israel, the Bible doesn't start with that group of people. The early focus is on individuals and families. We begin with the **"M"**. The M in "My" stands for **Mankind** found in Genesis 1-11. In these chapters, you do not find nations, but you will discover key figures like Adam and Eve, Cain and Abel, Seth, Enoch, Methuselah (the oldest man in the Bible) and Noah. We don't know how many years are covered in these chapters because we have no definitive evidence as to when it all started.

The Bible opens with, *"In the beginning God created the heavens and the earth"* (Genesis 1:1 – NV). No time is given. However, we are told about some specific events that occurred after "the beginning". Such events include man's fall into sin, God's judgment upon man by sending a world-wide flood, the spread of people groups from the three sons of Noah and the time when man no longer spoke just one language. God confused man's language and he was forced to find those of like language, resulting in people groups. The following chart of the first eleven chapters of Genesis is an overview of the Old Testament.

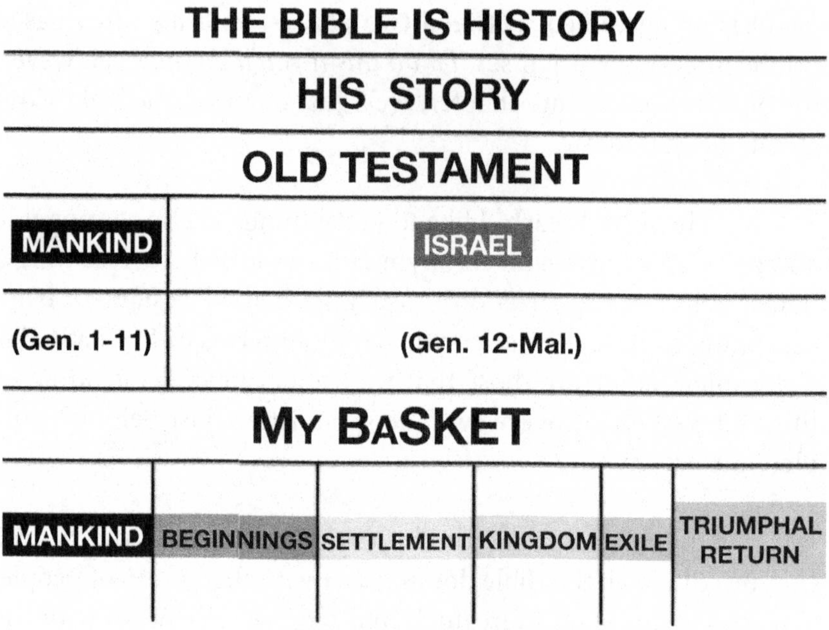

THE BIBLE IS HISTORY
HIS STORY
OLD TESTAMENT

MANKIND	ISRAEL
(Gen. 1-11)	(Gen. 12-Mal.)

MY BASKET

MANKIND	BEGINNINGS	SETTLEMENT	KINGDOM	EXILE	TRIUMPHAL RETURN

Figure 2 - Chart by Dr. Rick Yohn

Creation (Genesis 1-2)

There are many views concerning when the heavens and the earth were created. Was it in six literal 24-hour periods? Could it have been six long periods over millions of years? Perhaps God just spoke and all six-day periods occurred as He spoke the words consecutively. My purpose in this book is not to choose one view or another. I'll let that up to the theologians. However, we do know specific facts from the Genesis account.

Let's begin with the phrase, "God said." In other words, creation is the result of the will and spoken word of the Creator. He said, *"Let there be light,"* and there was light. Light originated from God the Creator, whether it took 24 hours for light to appear or longer, we can't be certain. But we can be assured that light would never have occurred, had God not said, *"Let there be light"*.

After God created, He rested. Was He exhausted? Does He get weary after working? Did He need the rest? No to all the above. He rested to set a precedent for each one of us. He gave us a six-day working week and then a day when we could rest. As the Creator, He knows that our bodies cannot function well on a seven-day working week. And when we violate times of rest, we do so at our own peril.

As we open the pages of Scripture, we are immediately confronted by the answer to the question scientists are still attempting to know. How did it all begin? How did time emerge from no time and material suddenly burst into being? Did someone start this process a long time ago, or did everything spontaneously emerge into what we call life?

The answer to those questions is profound and yet very simple if you are a person of faith – *"In the beginning God created the heavens and the earth"* (Genesis 1:1). We are not told if this occurred over a period of seconds, days, months, or decades. But we are informed that there was a beginning of time and matter that was birthed from an intelligent source that had no beginning. That intelligent source is known as "GOD".

Many of our political leaders, scientists, and university professors all adhere to the words penned by Thomas Jefferson in 1776 when he wrote, " *We hold these truths to be self-evident, that all men are **created equal**, that they are endowed by their **Creator** with certain unalienable Rights, that among these are Life, Liberty and the Pursuit of Happiness. That to secure these rights, Governments are instituted among Men, deriving their just powers from the consent of the governed"*[1], and yet at the same time these same individuals accept the theory of spontaneous evolution from existing matter and scoff at the idea of creation from an intelligent source.

The Bible tells us that there was a beginning of matter, light, an expanse between the waters, land, seas, vegetation, sun, moon and stars, living creatures of the sea and birds of the air, living creatures that move along the ground and wild animals *"according to their kind"* and finally man, whom God put in charge over His creation.

It's so difficult to imagine a time when there was no time, or a time when matter did not exist. We all have had a beginning and we all will have an end to this physical life, but the Creator had no beginning nor will He ever have an ending. Too much for the human mind to fathom. But we can know what He has revealed to us.

---

1. The United States Declaration of Independence.

GENESIS 1-11

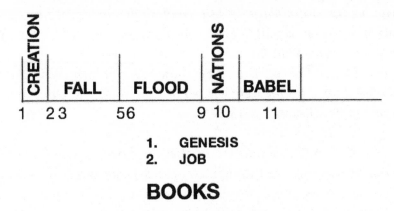

Figure 3 - Chart by Dr. Rick Yohn

Have you ever considered that creation is one expression of God's love language? Did you realize that the heavens speak? Listen to what the Psalmist tells us about the heavens: *"The heavens declare the glory of God; the skies proclaim the work of his hands. Day after day they pour forth speech; night after night they display knowledge. There is no speech or language where their voice is not heard. Their voice goes out into all the earth, their words to the ends of the world"* (Psalm 19:1-4).

Let's review those nouns and verbs again. David uses the three nouns of speech, language, and voice. Each of them is a description of communication. Then he adds the following verbs: declare, proclaim, pour forth, display, and heard. Again, words of communication. But what do the heavens tell us about this **"Lover of our soul"**?

First, they tell us that He is intelligent, for it took great intelligence to form so great and perfect a universe. It took intelligence to form our bodies in our mother's womb, as David so aptly describes it in one of his Psalms – *"For you created my inmost being; you knit me together in my mother's womb. I praise you because I am fearfully and wonderfully made; your works are wonderful, I know that full well. My frame was not hidden from you when I was made in the secret place. When I was woven together in the depths of the earth, your eyes saw my unformed body. All the days ordained for me were written in your book before one of them came to be"* (Psalm 139:13-16)

Secondly, we understand that this Lover is a God of order. Look at the universe through a large telescope and you see order. Look at a DNA sample through the microscope and you see perfect order. When God created the earth and the things in the earth, He declared each day, *"It is good"*. Then He created man and stated, *"It is very good"*. When you observe the days of creation, it reminds me of parents preparing to bring their first-born home from the hospital. They make sure the room is clean, the crib is put together, and the blankets are prepared to cover their precious gift from God. Everything is orderly for they want only the best for their new born.

Likewise, God had to get everything in order so that man could not only survive, but also enjoy life. Therefore, He begins by creating light. Then He calls for an expanse, known as "sky". This is followed by land, seas, vegetation, the sun and moon, stars, living creatures, creatures of the sea, birds, livestock, creatures that move along the ground, and wild animals. All of this was preparation for God's "new-born" that He called Man, including both male and female. He is an orderly Lover.

Thirdly, our Lover is a God of great power. Mankind uses the greatest power possible to send a satellite into orbit. We consider that as a great demonstration of man's ingenuity, knowledge, wisdom, and ability to harness power. But God is not in the business of "harnessing" power. He creates power, a power so strong that it creates something out of nothing. Many scientists claim that matter just came into existence all by itself, and they refuse to accept that an intelligent, orderly, and powerful God brought it all into existence. All the power that man has ever created can only be used to observe an infinitesimal particle of God's created universe.

Fourthly, the heavens also declare that our Lover is "glorious". David writes, *The heavens declare the "glory" of God*. God's glory is praiseworthy. Once again the Psalmist pens these descriptive words about the One who loves us, *"Oh Lord, our Lord, how majestic is your name in all the earth. You have set your glory above the heavens. . . When I consider your heavens, the work of your fingers, the moon and the stars, which you have set in place, what is man that you are mindful of him, the son of man that you care for him?"* (Psalm 8:1,3-4). Yes, this God who created us in His image is intelligent, orderly, powerful, and glorious. Now let's focus on our first two parents.

Adam & Eve

The Genesis account takes us to the beginning of man. The Bible names our first two parents as Adam and Eve. Though there are those who do not believe that Adam and Eve ever existed, I am convinced that they were two literal human beings created by God. After all, if you don't believe they ever existed, then you'll have a difficult time believing the Gospel of Luke, the Books of Acts, Romans, 1Corinthians, 1Timothy and Jude, because Luke, the Apostle Paul and Jude believed they existed and wrote about Adam.

They are the only two human beings that did not come into the world by natural birth. They were formed from the dust of the ground and Eve was created from a rib of Adam. They had everything going for them. They enjoyed a beautiful, pollution-free environment, not too hot and not too cold. They lived in perfect harmony with both the Creator and His creation. Adam even had the privilege of naming the animals. They had no worry about poisonous snakes, hungry tigers or alligators.

Everything in this creation was an expression of God's love for His creation in general and for mankind in particular. Before He created man, God made certain that man would be birthed into a beautiful environment. Everything was in place for His special creation. The best of food, friendship with animal life, beauty to enjoy, and finally a mate to love and cherish. God's love language for man and woman was expressed in His provision for each one of them.

And yet, a perfect environment, a perfect relationship with both Creator and creation plus all the delicious food within the Garden, our first parents still were not satisfied. They were convinced there must be something more. Something had to be better than perfection. And then one day they both fell for the lie of the centuries that would follow – *"You shall not die"*! How did that happen?

Satan entered the Garden and tempted Eve, who believed a lie and then gave the forbidden fruit to her husband to eat. What would cause Eve to fall away from God so quickly? The same things that cause all of us to get off the straight and narrow path.

Lie #1 – *"Did God really say. . .?"*[1] – The devil planted doubt in the mind of Eve.

---

1. Genesis 3:1

Today, skeptics do all they can to raise doubt about God's Word. *"Is this really God's Word?" "Can you truly trust your Bible?" "The Bible is full of contradictions."*

Lie #2 – *"You surely won't die."*[1] Today we believe that we won't get caught, no one will ever find out, or we can lie our way out of it if we're caught. In other words, *"Do what you want to do and don't worry about the consequences. Besides everyone else is doing it."* God told Adam that if he would eat from the tree of the knowledge of good and evil, he would die. Satan said that he wouldn't die. Which one was right? From that very day when Adam disobeyed God, the death process began. Sin was unleashed and death followed close behind. It took quite a while for the process to be completed, but Adam and Eve eventually died.

Lie #3 – *"You will be like God."*[2] We too often take the place of God in our everyday lives. We are convinced we know what is best for us. We believe that we can handle life well-enough on our own without God's help. We make decisions that we want to make whether they are good or bad decisions. And when we mess up our lives, we look for someone else to blame.

When Adam ate the fruit, which he knew was forbidden, sin penetrated our human race. And from that moment on, man has been separated from God and desperately needs to be reconciled with God, or brought back into a renewed relationship with Him. In His mercy and love, God made a provision to cover Adam and Eve's sin, and later provided a system by which all mankind could be reconciled to God. Animals were sacrificed as a substitute for man's sin. The Bible clearly states the need for blood to be shed so that sin might be forgiven - *"In fact, the law requires that*

---

1. Genesis 3:4
2. Genesis 3:5

nearly everything be cleansed with blood, and without the shedding of blood there is no forgiveness" (Hebrews 9:22 – NIV).

Next, we move from creation to the fall of man. But though man rebelled against God, resulting in his expulsion from the Garden of Eden, God continued to want a relationship with the man and woman, so He blessed Adam and Eve with two sons, Cain and Abel.

That one bite of the fruit changed the course of this love story from God. Youth and beauty turned to aging, along with the side effects which accompany the process: Loss of hearing, lessening of sight, sickness, disease, anger, hatred, murder, continuous conflict between individuals, families and nations. Harmony turned to disharmony. Unity turned into division. Love turned to hate. Trust morphed into suspicion.

God could have walked away from the entire situation, destroyed all mankind and started all over again. But God's character would not allow abandonment. Unknown to man, God had already prepared a loving plan that would work. We addressed it earlier and call it "**REDEMPTION**", which includes the following benefits: a purchasing of something, a paying a price for something, a substitution (one person for another) and a setting free from bondage.

Adam and Eve's sin against God did not take Him off-guard. He was saddened, but not astonished. God the Father and His Son, Jesus Christ, had already decided on a plan of action, not "**IF**" man sinned against Him, but "**WHEN**" man sinned against God.

Within this plan, God was preparing our substitute, an individual who would accept the penalty for our sin. One who would be like a lamb going to the slaughter by paying the price of sin with His own life. But that's another story.

Cain & Abel

Sin's effects took place immediately in the aging process of Adam and Eve. And then it sprang into full force after their sons, Cain and Abel were born and had grown into manhood. Cain was a farmer and Abel was a shepherd. Each year they would bring an offering to God. Behind this story is the assumption that the message given to Adam and Eve and demonstrated by God through the provision of garments (necessitating the death of one or more animals) had been passed down to both sons.

When Cain brought his offering to God, he brought forth an offering from the soil. On the other hand, Abel brought forth an offering from his livestock. Cain's offering demonstrated the work of man, while Abel's offering conveyed that blood had been shed and God's process for forgiveness of sin had been followed. The result – God accepted Abel's offering and rejected Cain's offering.

At that point, Cain had a decision to make. He needed to recognize that he had brought the wrong type of offering to God and was expected either to come back with a lamb, or carry out his jealous feelings towards his brother. God challenged Cain, for He knew what was going through Cain's mind. Therefore, he appeared to him and raised the following questions – *"Why are you angry? Why is your face downcast? If you do what is right, will you not be accepted? But if you do not do what is right, sin is crouching at your door; it desires to have you, but you must master it"* (Genesis 4:6-7). Cain made the latter choice and we now suffer the consequences: *"Therefore, just as sin entered the world through one man, and death through sin, and in this way death came to all men, because all sinned – for before the law was given, sin was in the world"* (Romans 5:12-13).

Cain's jealousy drove him to murder his brother, Abel, and his family was torn apart. Cain left his home and went out from the presence of the Lord, moving east of Eden. There he built a city and the lifestyle of those in the line of Cain was one of living outside the presence of the Lord. But God was gracious to Adam and Eve and gave them another son, Seth.

The Line Of Seth

ENOCH - As you continue to read Genesis you can trace the line of Seth and that of Cain. Those in the line of Seth called on the name of the Lord, while those in Cain's line walked away from God. Those in the lineage of Seth accepted the love God was offering them. From the line of Seth came godly men such as **Enoch**. The Bible tells us, *"Enoch walked with God; then he was no more, because God took him away"* (Genesis 5:24). We are not told how God took Enoch away, but most commentators believe that he was one of two men who did not experience death, the other being Elijah.

METHUSELAH - Another man who came from the line of Seth was Methuselah. We also don't know a lot about him, but since he lived 969 years, he holds the record for the longest life. As the years passed, man became so corrupt that God decided to bring a world- wide flood upon all men, except for a man named **Noah** and his family, who were also from the line of Seth.

NOAH (Genesis 6) – The Scriptures inform us that Noah found grace in the eyes of the Lord and did everything God told him to do, including building an ark for his family and the animals. God's grace is another expression of His love. God told Noah to take seven of every kind of clean animal, a male and its mate, and two of every kind of unclean animal into the ark (Genesis 7:2-3).

Following God's orders, Noah worked on that ark over many years. Finally, one day the darkness of the heavens shut out all light. Only when lightning shot through the sky could a man see his own hands. Then the thunder blasted through the sky and was enough to break a man's eardrums. As Noah led the last of the animals into the ark, God shut the door and the rains poured down in torrents and the springs burst their seams. Forty days and nights passed and then the rain stopped, but the flood continue to build. One hundred and ten days passed before Noah could open the door and release the animals and his family.

My Three Sons (Genesis 10)

Noah's wife gave birth to three sons named Ham, Shem and Japheth. When God confused the languages at Babel, the Hamites move towards the southwest, the Semites moved east and the Japhites moved north.

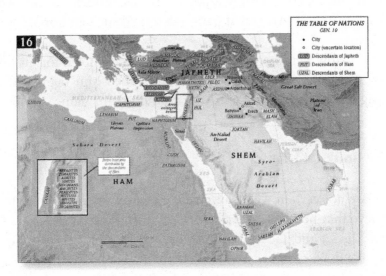

Figure 4 - THE TABLE OF NATIONS - Briscoe, Thomas V. 1998. Nashville, TN: Holman Bible Atlas, 37.

Babel (Genesis 11)

All mankind still spoke one language. However, though God showed His love to mankind by sparing a family through the flood, man disobeyed God once again. The Lord told Noah to multiply and replenish the earth. Mankind multiplied, but decided that his plan was better than God's plan, so he decided to stay in the land of Shinar (present day Iraq-Iran). There he would build a worship center, develop his own religion and remain where he was.

Rejected love from God often results in negative consequences, as the Lord attempts to restore man to Himself. Therefore, God once again intervened and this time He struck the people with diverse languages, so they could no longer effectively communicate with one another, resulting in the scattering of Noah's three sons to various parts of the known world. No longer was communication as easy as previously. And no longer was God going to deal only with individuals to carry out His will. He was now ready to communicate His love to mankind through another avenue, which we call a nation. And what nation deserved such an honor? None!

However, there was one man who was known for his integrity. Even God looked upon him and called him blameless and upright. We find him in the Book that bears his name – **JOB**.

The Book Of Job

We are not certain when Job lived. However, most commentators believe that he lived either before or during the patriarchs: Abraham, Isaac, and Jacob. Furthermore, most Bible scholars believe that the Book of Job was written before the book of Genesis because Moses is the writer of Genesis and Job lived many years prior to Moses.

This Book can be divided into three major sections: (1) Job's life of tranquility; (2) Job's attempt to answer the question "**WHY**"; (3) Job's "A-HA" moment.

As the book unfolds, life could not have been better. God blessed him with seven children, an envious reputation within his town and among his friends, and great wealth. But when the devil entered the presence of God, he asked permission to afflict Job greatly. The devil was convinced that he could cause Job to turn his back on God. The Lord allowed Satan to afflict Job by removing much of that which formed his reputation, but would not allow the devil to take Job's life. However, Satan did take Job's wealth, children, and health, but failed to seize Job's integrity.

This great man of God was devastated. Not only did he lose everything, but his wife was so emotionally overcome that she told him to curse God and die. Such a response is certainly understandable because her security was ripped from her heart. And the children she loved so dearly were gone. And yet in the midst of all this loss, Job was able to say, *"Naked I came from my mother's womb, and naked I will depart. The Lord gave and the Lord has taken away; may the name of the Lord be praised."* (Job 2:10) Furthermore, when Job's wife told him to curse God and die, he responded by saying, *"Shall we accept good from God, and not trouble?"* (Job 2:10)

From that point forward, Job raised the question, "**WHY?**" This would be a very normal response of all of us if we found ourselves in that situation. In the next chapter, Job asked that question five times. Why, why, why, why, why? As Job was crying out to God with the **"Why?"** question, his three friends arrived and attempted to answer that question for him. Then the Q & A process continued up to chapter 38, but came to a complete halt when God stepped into the discussion. God responded to this interaction between friends by throwing out a series of questions himself.

1. Where were you when I laid the earth's foundation?
2. What is the way to the abode of light? And where does darkness reside?
3. Who endowed the heart with wisdom or gave understanding to the mind?
4. Who provides food for the raven when its young cry out to God and wander about for lack of food?
5. Does the eagle soar at your command and build his nest on high?
6. Who has a claim against me that I must pay? Everything under heaven belongs to me.

These are only six of the many questions that God asked Job. I imagine that Job sat in total silence throughout that questioning. His jaw must have dropped after the very first question. Stunned, Job admitted to God, *"Surely I spoke of things I did not understand, things too wonderful for me to know."* (Job 42:3) And then Job concluded with these words, *"My ears had heard of you but now my eyes have seen you. Therefore, I despise myself and repent in dust and ashes"* (Job 42:5).

Notice that God never answered the why question which was attempted to be answered by Job and his three friends. We all tend to question God during times of confusion and great difficulty. But the questions we normally raise are "WHY?" "HOW?" and "WHEN?" Sometimes God answers those questions. But in this book, he answered none of them. The reason for this is that he wanted his friends to know **"WHO?"** When God questioned Job, He raised the **"WHO?"** question 25 times. And that question was answered resoundingly.

We might ask ourselves, *"Where is God's love in all of this?"* Despite his troubles and great loss, Job could still see the love of God. He cried out to His Lord, *"You have granted me life and steadfast love, and your care has preserved my spirit."* (Job 10:12).

We want to know, *"Why would a loving God allow these things to happen to a very faithful man of God?"* But from God's perspective the important issue is, *"Who is in control of the situation?"* We either interpret God by looking at life's events, or we interpret life's events by looking through the lens of the word of God.

However, though Job was a man who loved God and maintained his integrity, he was the exception. Though one could find a few individuals who loved God, the various people groups were corrupt.

Therefore, God had to create a new nation. So, the Lord went to a pagan culture in a pagan land and chose a man and his family for a new responsibility. God showed favor to the family of a man named Terah. Who is he? The next chapter answers that question.

CHAPTER

3

Love Through a Nation

Now that we've glimpsed creation and our original parents with their offspring, rather than walk through Scripture by providing a synopsis of all sixty-six books, it would be better to focus on some key people whom God used to spread His Story to their generation. Therefore, we will look at both the Old and New Testaments through both a biographical and a chronological lens, beginning with Genesis 12 through the Book of Revelation. We begin with the nation of Israel.

This people group would be known by different names as time passed. They would be called Hebrews and later Israel, along with the name Jews. Though we move into a new section of the Bible, we're still in the Book of Genesis. At the end of chapter eleven, we are introduced to a man by the name of Terah. And from Genesis 12 to the end of Malachi (the last Old Testament Book) the focus will be on this one nation, Israel. All the other nations mentioned throughout the Old Testament are presented in relation to how they interact, invade or partner with the nation of Israel.

Terah

Who was Terah? He was a man who lived in Ur, the largest city in the world four thousand years ago which is now in present day Iraq. There are two possible locations for Ur. One is about two hundred miles southeast of modern Baghdad. The other possibility is located northwest of the modern city of Mosul, formally known as the Old Testament city of Nineveh. He had a wife and three sons named Abram, Nahor and Haran. There was nothing special about this family. No one had done anything outstanding at the time. They were just a family of five, living like everyone else around them. However, they were also worshipers of other gods.

While still in Ur, God called Abram to leave his country, people and father's household and go to a place God would eventually show him. During that time, Terah's youngest son, Haran, died. Due to Abram's calling from God and Haran's death, Terah moved his family from Ur to Haran. They lived in that city until Terah died. Now it was Abram's turn to complete his journey and fully obey God's call on his life.

The Patriarchs (Fathers of Israel)

ABRAM (ABRAHAM)

We don't know if God appeared in person or not, but He somehow communicated with Abram that he was to leave the city of Haran and go to the place that God would later show him.

Try to put yourself into the shoes (sandals) of Abram. You are minding your own business when one day you either hear a voice or experience a very strong impression that it's time to pack up and leave the country of your origin and go to another country, though you are not sure where that country is located. But as

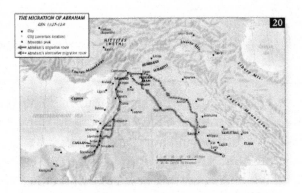

Figure 5 - Briscoe, Thomas V. 1998. Nashville, TN: Holman Bible Atlas, p.46

Abram obeys, God speaks to him more and more, providing other instructions to what seems to be a scavenger hunt.

However, leaving their present location is not all there was to that God-encounter. There's more. God makes some very specific promises to Abram and asks for nothing in return. That's very unusual. It wasn't like other covenants that say, *"If you do this, I'll do that"*. It was a one-way communication.

- I will make you into a great nation
- I will bless you
- I will make your name great
- You will be a blessing
- I will bless those who bless you and whoever curses you I will curse
- All the peoples on earth will be blessed through you (Genesis 12:1-3)

REALLY? Abram must have wondered, *"Who am I, that God should do so much for me? And who is this God? I've never met him before. Can I trust Him to do what He has promised me? What if I just dreamed this? How can I check whether this is real?"* But such questions did not stop Abram from responding in obedience.

"By faith, Abraham, when called to go to a place he would later receive as his inheritance, obeyed and went, even though he did not know where he was going" (Hebrews 11:8).

Now it's not unusual to launch out in some venture and not know where you would end up. Most financial investments are made on such speculation and hope, and sometimes those decisions prove disastrous. But Abram's case was different. He was placing his trust and confidence in this new God who either appeared to him or spoke to him out of the blue, and Abram believed that this God would fulfill His promise. That took a lot of faith. What next?

Abram informed his wife, Sarai and nephew, Lot, what the next steps would be. They all left Haran and made their way towards the south, which brings us to our section on Beginnings. Recall that the first part of our acronym was **My BaSKET**. The M stands for **Mankind**. Now we will look at the B in Basket.

The **B** in Basket is for the **Beginnings** of the nation of Israel. This section includes the entire first five books of the Bible, which have several names. The Greek name for this collection of books is Pentateuch, at times translated as five vessels. . .five containers. . .five-volume book. The Hebrews (Jews) had two names for this collection. The first name is "The Law of Moses" because these books contain the life, history and laws that God gave to Moses after he brought the Hebrews out of Egyptian slavery. The name used today by the Jews is The Torah (The Law). In Jesus' day, the Old Testament was divided into three parts: The Law of Moses, The Prophets and The Writings.[1] There are several key individuals throughout this section including the Patriarchs (Fathers) – Abraham, Isaac, Jacob and Joseph. In this chapter, we'll explore these four individuals and their contribution to A Love Story From God.

---

1. Luke 24:44

Abraham

The Bible introduces us to this man in Genesis 12 with what is known as the **Abrahamic Covenant**, an agreement that God made unilaterally with Abraham. I personally believe that this Covenant is unconditional. In other words, God does not say, *"If you do this, I'll do that".* God placed no conditions on Abram. The Lord just told Him, *"I will . . . I will. . . I will . . . I will . . .".* Let's look at this Covenant as God made it known to Abram.

I love the way the promises of this Covenant unfold. You've seen the ads on television where the announcer shows you an item that he wants you to believe you desperately need. He then informs you that you can get it for only $19.95. Then he adds, *"But that's not all, there's more".* He then throws in another item or tells you that you can get a second thing-a-ma-jig without any more expense other than the shipping and handling (which is where they make their money).

Well, though God wasn't selling anything to Abram, these promises begin in Genesis 12 and then it's as if God adds, *"but that's not all, there's more."* He then includes a few more promises in Genesis 13 and adds another, *"but that's not all, there's more."* You turn to Genesis 15 and God once again adds, *"but that's not all, there's more."* Finally, in Genesis 17 the Lord begins to narrow the scope of all these blessings.

Genesis 12 - We've already covered His promises in Genesis 12: (1) **A great nation**; (2) A **great name**; (3) A **blessing to many**; (4) **Bless** those who bless you and **curse** those who curse you; and (5) All peoples of the earth will be **blessed through you**. Those five blessings in themselves would overwhelm anybody. What could you add to that list? Let me count the ways.

Genesis 13 – A great Land! *"Lift up your eyes from where you are and look north and south, east and west. All the land that you see I will give to you and your offspring forever"*. Abram was a stranger in a strange land. This land had strange customs and most likely even a strange language. The landscape was unfamiliar. The dress of the people was different. They worshipped gods unknown to Abraham. And their worship included practices that even made Abram blush. But God promised him that one-day, this entire land would belong to Abram's offspring. And speaking of offspring, here's another, *"but that's not all, there's more"*.

A great people! *"I will make your offspring like the dust of the earth, so that if anyone could count the dust, then your offspring could be counted"*. Why would this seem to be so overwhelming to Abram? He had no child. His wife, Sarai, was barren. Furthermore, she was up in age and so was he. Abram was 75 years old. That promise seemed more impossible than the first six promises. As time passed and Sarai was still barren, Abram became more and more concerned. Did he misread God's intentions? Could he possibly have misunderstood what God had promised when it came to his offspring? *"But that's not all, there's more"*!

A Son from Abram's Own Body - More years passed and still no children. Abram became concerned that perhaps he was just dreaming. He wanted children so badly. Could he have just imagined the whole thing? He finally lays it all out before the Lord and cries out, *"O Sovereign Lord, what can you give me since I remain childless and the one who will inherit my estate is Eliezer of Damascus . . . You have given me no children; so a servant in my household will be my heir"* (Genesis 15:2-3). His concern and doubting are understandable. Abram's lack of children greatly distressed him. And it's often at the place of our utter helplessness that God comes through so powerfully. Listen to God's wonderful response – *"This man will not be your heir, but a son coming from* *your own body will be your heir"* (Genesis 15:4). Then God takes Abram outside and tells him to look up at the stars and attempt to count them. As many stars that he sees will equal the number of offspring he will have (Genesis 15:5).

Now here's the clincher. The next few words are repeated several times throughout Scripture. *"Abram believed the Lord, and he credited it to him as righteousness"* (Genesis 15:6). Why is that sentence so important that it is repeated in Romans 4:3; Galatians 3:6; and James 2:23? The reason is because it introduces a very important theological term known as **"justification"**. And what is justification?

Justification is the concept that means there is a God who is loving, just (He does not overlook sin) and righteous (He is Himself without sin). This God declared that Abram was righteous because he believed the promise that God made to him, even though his wife was barren. Today, when we believe what God says is true, we also experience this "justification". No, God is not promising any of us offspring, but He does give us another promise, which is His most powerful expression of love – *"For God so loved the world that he gave his one and only Son, that whoever believes in him shall not perish but have eternal life"* (John 3:16). Today, we place our total confidence in the promise that Jesus died for our sins and paid the penalty of death in our place. When we believe that truth, God promises us that He has transferred our sin to His Son Jesus and at the same time, He has transferred Jesus' righteousness to us. This transaction provides salvation for those of us who believe in God's promise and God's way.

Where can we find the proof of this transaction? Listen to the words of the Apostle Paul when he writes, *"God made him who had no sin to be sin for us, so that in him we might become the righteousness of God"* (2Corinthians 5:21).

Now let's continue our exploration of God's Covenant with Abram.

Genesis 15 – The Covenant Is Ratified

Whenever a covenant or agreement was made between two parties, there was usually some type of ceremony or event that ratified or sealed that agreement. Though God had made these promises to Abram, no such ceremony had yet occurred. But when we turn to Genesis 15, we see that event unfold.

God first informs Abram that his offspring will be enslaved for four hundred years. But God will deliver them from slavery and they will leave with great wealth. And when they do experience this physical deliverance (redemption), they will come to where God was speaking with Abram, the Land of Promise, present day Israel. (Genesis 15:13-16). Then God makes His promise official through, what is often called a "blood covenant".

God told Abram to get a heifer, a goat and a ram, a dove and a young pigeon. Abram cut them in two and laid each half opposite one another so the blood could drain into a ditch. Then Abram fell into a deep sleep and a thick and dreadful darkness came over him. The event continues - *"When the sun had set and darkness had fallen, a smoking firepot with a blazing torch appeared and passed between the pieces. On that day the Lord made a covenant with Abram . . ."* (Genesis 15:17-18a). Notice that Abram was sound asleep. He had nothing to do with the covenant. However, God, in the form of a torch, passed through the blood, between the pieces of sacrifice, indicating that He will unilaterally fulfill the promises of the covenant to Abram and his offspring. Then God added the dimensions of the land He will give Abram and his offspring (Genesis 15:18-21). The story continues . . .

ISHMAEL - When Abram was in his late 80's, he and Sarai panicked. She told him to go to her handmaiden and have a son through her. Abram listened to his wife and the result was a son named Ishmael. By all customs and rights, Ishmael should have received all the blessings of a firstborn son. However, God appeared to Abram when he was ninety-nine years old and told him that the son of promise would come from both his and Sarah's bodies. God promised, *"Yes, but your wife Sarah will bear you a son, and you will call him Isaac. I will establish my covenant with him as an everlasting covenant for his descendants after him"* (Genesis 17:19).

Abram's name is now changed to Abraham – the father of many nations. Not only did Isaac come from him, resulting in the nation of Israel, but also Ishmael came from Abraham and all the nations that claim Ishmael as their father. Eventually Sarah died and Abraham married Keturah and had sons through her, which resulted in other nations.

Before I introduce you to Abraham's son, Isaac, let's do a little review. Which promises were fulfilled over these years? (1) Abraham became a great nation (Israel); (2) God greatly blessed Abraham; (3) Abraham was a blessing to others; (4) God blessed those who blessed Abraham (Israel) and cursed those who cursed Abraham (Israel) – many nations and organizations have wanted to wipe Israel from the face of the earth, but they become defeated themselves (Babylonians, Medes and Persians, Greece, Rome, Arabs, Turks, Germans, ISIS, Hezbollah, etc.); (5) All peoples of the earth have been blessed through Abraham (via Jesus, the distant son of Abraham); (6) Abraham's descendants are as numerous as the stars in the sky (Jews, Muslims & Christians); (7) Israel now lives in the Land that God promised Abraham, though more is promised than what they now possess.

Isaac

The Scriptures don't tell us a lot about Isaac, other than he was the one God had chosen all along to be the heir of the promises God had given to Abraham. Sarah had died and Isaac was still without a wife, so Abraham asked his servant to go back to Haran and find a wife for his son, Isaac. The Lord guided the servant to Rebekah, the daughter of Abraham's brother, Nahor. She traveled the long journey from Haran to Canaan with Abraham's servant, married Isaac and they had twin boys: Esau and Jacob. Before the boys were born, God told Isaac and Rebekah that the older (Esau) would serve the younger (Jacob). That concept was totally against the culture of the day, but it is exactly what happened. From Esau came the Edomites and from Jacob came the Israelites. In fact, the name "Israel" was the name that God gave to Jacob after Jacob wrestled with God (Genesis 35:10).

Between the two sons, we probably would have chosen Esau over Jacob. Esau was a man's man, a hunter and a rugged individual. Jacob was a conniver and a Mama's boy. Esau was the favorite son of Isaac and Jacob was the favorite son of Rebekah. Choosing favorites among your children is a great way to develop a dysfunctional family. Eventually Jacob deceived his father and received his father's blessing and then stole the birthright from his brother Esau. Esau was so angry that he planned to kill his brother, so Jacob fled for his life to Haran. There he met Rachael and fell in love with her. However, her father Laban was also a deceiver and tricked Jacob into first marrying his older daughter Leah. Then after working for Laban another seven years, his uncle gave him permission to marry Rachael, who was the love of his life.

Immediately a rivalry developed between the two sisters. And what would you expect? Leah started to produce children, but Rachael was barren. She followed Sarah's misguided idea and told Jacob to have a child by her handmaid, Bilhah. When her sister Leah saw what Rachel had done, she asked Jacob to sleep with her handmaid, Zilpah. This whole fiasco eventually ended with 12 sons for Jacob by four different women. You may have heard about the 12 tribes of Israel. We'll meet the family from where the tribes originated. Leah (wife #1) had four sons: Reuben, Simeon, Levi and Judah. Bilhah (Handmaid to Rachael) had two sons: Dan and Naphtali. Zilpah (handmaid to Leah) had two sons: Gad and Asher. Then Leah had three more children: Issachar, Zebulun and a daughter named Dinah. Rachael (wife #2, but the one Jacob truly loved) finally gave birth to Joseph and eventually to Benjamin before she died.

Joseph

Often when people refer to the "Patriarchs", they refer to Abraham, Isaac and Jacob. However, this eleventh son, Joseph plays a major part in the life of God's love story and the people of Israel. We are introduced to him when he was only seventeen years of age.

We can better understand the underlying animosity when we realize two very important facts: (1) When Joseph was born, he came into a family of ten older brothers. He was the runt, the youngest of eleven and hated by his brothers. They observed him growing up and watched their father show special attention and favor to Joseph. Everything came to a head when Joseph was seventeen. Joseph could have sung Frank Sinatra's popular rendition – *"When I was seventeen, it was a very good year. . ."*. For Joseph, it was great. His dad loved him, showed him favoritism and made a very special garment for him that became the envy of all his brothers. On top of that, Joseph had two interesting dreams that he just had to share with the rest of his brothers.

Dream #1 – *"Listen to this dream I had: We were binding sheaves of grain out in the field when suddenly my sheaf rose and stood upright, while your sheaves gathered around mine and bowed down to it"* (Genesis 37:6-7)

Brothers' Response – *"Do you intend to reign over us? Will you actually rule us?"* (Genesis 37:8) They hated him even more.

Now you would think that the kid would finally get it. *"I'm hated by my brothers. And when I told them about my dream, I could see it in their eyes. They were seething with hate. I'd better keep my mouth shut and keep my dreams to myself."* That may have been the wisest course of action, but remember that Joseph was a teenager. Aren't we told that the brains of teens are not fully developed? They don't seem to put cause and effect together in their thought process. Such was the brain and wisdom of Joseph.

He had a second dream and decided that this one also had to be shared with his brothers. After all, Joseph is the "Johnny-come-lately". He's the last one up to bat. He's the kid who always wants to tag along with his older siblings and can become an embarrassment to their friends. So, our dreamer rushed to his older brothers and dumped another load on them.

Dream #2 – *"Listen,' he said, 'I had another dream, and this time the sun and moon and eleven stars were bowing down to me"* (Genesis 37:9). In fact, Joseph thought this dream was so fantastic that he decided to share it with his father, who rebuked him.

Jacob's Reaction – *"What is this dream you had? Will your mother and I and your brothers actually come and bow down to the ground before you?"* (Genesis 37:10)

The Brothers' Reaction – *"His brothers were jealous of him. . ."* (Genesis 37:11).

Jealousy led to greater and deeper anger until it hit a boiling point. The brothers made a fateful decision. Joseph had to go. They plotted to kill him and they would have, had it not been for the intervention of Judah. He knew that they would be answerable to their father, Jacob. Therefore, Judah convinced his brothers to throw Joseph into a well, while they ate and plotted the next step.

While they were eating the ten brothers saw a group of Ishmaelite travelers on their way to Egypt. Great! Now the plot comes into focus. *"Let's sell Joseph to these strangers, kill an animal and douse the garment in the blood and then tell Dad that a ferocious animal must have killed his favorite son. Sounds like a plan."*

Decision made. The ten brothers sold Joseph to strangers traveling to Egypt and then returned home to tell their father the concocted story of a wild animal killing Joseph. Of course, their father was devastated, convinced that he had lost his youngest son to some ferocious animal. But the plot thickens when the youngest son was sold as a slave to a wealthy Egyptian, but was then unjustly accused of adultery with his master's wife and soon thrown in prison. And then something happened in the prison that forever changed the life of Joseph and his entire family.

Joseph was in prison for something he never committed. Several years passed and the Pharaoh had a dream that demanded someone to interpret it for him, but none of his wise counselors could do so. Eventually his cupbearer remembered that there was a young man in prison who could do just that. Pharaoh ordered Joseph to be brought to him and God helped Joseph interpret the dream.

Pharaoh was so impressed with Joseph's ability that he made him number two in the kingdom – *"Since God has made all this known to you, there is no one so discerning and wise as you. You shall be in charge of my palace, and all my people are to submit to your orders. Only with respect to the throne will I be greater than you"* (Genesis 41:39-40).

In the meantime, a great famine hit the land of Israel, so Jacob sent his sons down to Egypt to buy grain. When they arrived, they were brought into the presence of Joseph and bowed down to him, not knowing before whom they were bowing. However, Joseph immediately recognized his brothers. Recognizing that the tables had now been turned in his favor, Joseph decided to see how they would react to a false accusation. He then accused them of being spies, demanding that they bring to him the youngest son, Benjamin. And to guarantee their return, Joseph had Simeon taken from them and bound before their eyes.[1]

When the brothers returned to Jacob, they had to break the bad news that his son, Simeon was left behind. Jacob went into a deep depression, convinced that he now had lost another son. As time passed, the famine grew greater, so Jacob finally sent his sons back to Egypt, only this time, young Benjamin went with them.

When Joseph saw his brothers, he broke down crying loudly. Joseph finally revealed his identity to the astonishment and fear of his brothers. But he assured them that he would not kill them. In fact, his years of rejection and imprisonment developed him into a much wiser, humble individual. He was now able to see the hand of God in everything that happened to him.

---

1. Genesis 42

Though Joseph had the power and all the reasons in the world to get even with his brothers, he ran to them, threw his arms around them and cried. Then he spoke these compassionate and forgiving words – *"So then, it was not you who sent me here, but God. He made me father to Pharaoh, lord of his entire household and ruler of all Egypt"* (Genesis 45:8). After staying in Egypt for a short while, the brothers returned to their father Jacob with the overwhelmingly good news. *"Joseph is alive and he is number two in command in the land of Egypt"*!

Jacob couldn't believe his ears. *"Is this some kind of a cruel joke? Are you leveling with me? You say that my son Joseph is alive? And he ranks just under Pharaoh in the land of Egypt? This is too much. I must sit down!"*

Once the shock left him, Jacob and his household packed their belongings, went to Egypt and lived there until Jacob died. And after the death of their father, Joseph reminded his brothers, *"Don't be afraid. Am I in the place of God? You intended to harm me, but God intended it for good to accomplish what is now being done, the saving of many lives. So then, don't be afraid. I will provide for you and your children.' 'And he reassured them and spoke kindly to them"'* (Genesis 50:19-21).

Imagine forgiving someone who hated you and did everything possible to make life miserable for you. That type of reaction is not natural. It's supernatural. Without seeing life through the eyes of God, we would never come to Joseph's conclusion. We wouldn't see any good in being rejected by our siblings or have false accusations thrown against our character or being put in prison for something we had never done. We would probably have to be a great optimist or we'd have to capture God's perspective as it's recorded by the Apostle Paul in the Book of Romans – *"And we know that in all things God works for the good of those who love him, who have been called according to his purpose"* (Romans 8:28). But that's not all, there's more.

Though this ends God's love story through the Patriarchs of Israel, the Beginnings of Israel continues into the next chapter. That is where we are going to discover how God fulfilled his promise to Abraham when He said that Abraham's offspring would grow so numerous that the nation in which they live will enslave them. And yet, the Lord would bring them out of slavery to the place where God was speaking to Abraham

4

Love in Tough Times

How the mighty are fallen! He had fame, fortune, power and a position envied by many. This man came from Boston, MA, went to Brown University, got a law degree and started his own law firm. He later went into politics and was asked by the President of the United States to be his Special Council. In his own words, he said, *"Here I am sitting in the office next to the President of the United States. Walking in and out of his office everyday of the week. One of the most powerful positions of the world. Limousines outside waiting for me. Admirals and Generals saluting. Everything a person could want and, curiously enough, that was the first time in my life that I felt empty"* (chuckcolsonstory.com). How could a man feel empty when he held a position that most of us would envy? He wouldn't find that out for a few more years.

Chuck was known for being ruthless, with a taking no prisoners mentality. The press at the time of the Watergate Scandal during the Presidency of Richard M. Nixon called this man "Nixon's Hatchet Man". His name was Charles Colson. Though he was a well-educated New Englander, a brilliant lawyer and an ex-marine, he was now on his way to prison. Imagine, the Special

Counsel to the President was headed for prison and President Richard M. Nixon himself resigned as President of the United States. How the mighty have fallen! The President went on to a life of writing books and in a strange way became a statesman in political circles. What about Colson?

It's true that Colson fell from fame, fortune, power and position to wearing a prison outfit stamped with a number. But that's not the end of the story. A short time before he went to prison, he visited a friend who talked to him about his need of a Savior. That was an eye-opener for Colson. At first, he couldn't believe his ears. His friend was the President of a large organization and had himself once been just like Colson, greatly focused, hard lined with a take-no-prisoners mode of operation. And now his friend was talking to him about Jesus. Eventually Chuck Colson cried out to God, invited Christ into his life, went to prison, began a prayer meeting and Bible study with other prisoners, and eventually founded Prison Fellowship, a ministry to prisoners that has changed the lives of thousands of those convicted of various crimes.

Not many people fall from such great heights, hit bottom and find the true meaning of life in a personal relationship with the Creator. Chuck Colson is a 21st Century example. But there is another man who had a similar experience as Mr. Colson. He too enjoyed power, fame, riches and a very high position that gave him access to the ruler of his day. He too was well educated, and was powerful in speech and action (Acts 7:22). But one day he murdered another man and fled for his life to a distant land. Like Chuck Colson, he fell from being a great "somebody" to the depths of becoming a "nobody". In his new-found land, he met a young girl, married her and began working for her father. Great job? Not at all.

We might wonder why God would ever chose a murder to accomplish anything significant. As I've ministered over the years, I've been amazed at some of the people God chose to accomplish His purpose. The man that I'm talking about was once a Prince in the Royal Family of Egypt. And now? He was a lonely, unrecognized shepherd. At one time, heads of state would bow before him. Now, even the sheep paid him little respect. But like Colson, this man they called Moses, had an encounter with God. It wasn't a friend telling him how to experience a meaningful life, but rather a burning bush that wasn't consumed by the fire.

One day as Moses was tending his sheep he noticed a blazing bush. At first, he paid little attention because the heat of the desert could spontaneously set bushes on fire. But this bush wasn't consumed. Moses inquisitively went over to see the strange phenomenon. As he approached the bush, he heard a voice coming from the bush saying, *"Moses, Moses"!* That day changed the life of this man, as well as millions of other lives down through the ages.

Who was behind that voice? The Creator of the universe. The same God who had made Himself known and expressed His love to mankind time and again. This God introduced Himself to Moses as Yahweh or Jehovah. No one truly knows the exact pronunciation of this word because the Hebrews had no vowels in their alphabet. The 22-letter alphabet was all consonants. There was no a-e-i-o-u. The name is composed of four Hebrew letters (YHWH, HVHY) and can be translated, "I Am". In other words, God is the self-existing God. He needs no counsel or help from anyone. Furthermore, He is also the All-Sufficient God. This was the special name by which He wanted to be known by the nation of Israel. It is the name that Jesus called Himself when talking with the religious leaders of His day – *"I tell you the truth,' Jesus answered, 'before Abraham was born, I am'"!* (YHWH) (John 8:58). The Jewish leaders recognized that with this statement, Jesus was making Himself equal with the *"I Am"* of the Old Testament. Their response was to pick up stones to stone Him.

In this encounter, God not only made Himself known to Moses, but also informed him that, like a loving parent, He heard His people cry out for deliverance and that He was about to raise up someone to deliver them. Moses had attempted to do that forty years earlier, resulting in taking the life of an Egyptian and fleeing for his own life. Now he learned that God had a different plan. God revealed His plan to Moses, and to Moses' shock, that plan included him. God's plan for Moses included, *"I am sending you to Pharaoh to bring my people the Israelites out of Egypt"* (Exodus 3:10), Moses stood before God in unbelief. *"Me? You want me to go back to Egypt and confront Pharaoh?"*

God's love for the people on earth included a message of forgiveness. He wanted the world to know the extent of His love (breadth, width, height, and depth). It is a love that is never turned off and on due to rejection. The only condition is that it needs to be received and enjoyed. It is a love that is so strong, once a person receives it, such love cannot be removed.

The Apostle Paul expands on the quality of God's love when he writes, *"Who shall separate us from the love of Christ? Shall trouble or hardship or persecution or famine or nakedness or danger or sword?"* He then adds, *"For I am convinced that neither death nor life, neither angels nor demons, neither the present nor the future, nor any powers, neither height nor depth nor anything else in al creation, will be able to separate us from the love of God that is in Christ Jesus our Lord"*
(Romans 8:35,38-39)

He immediately went into high gear, thinking up one excuse after another, but God turned a deaf ear to all of Moses' excuses. His last excuse was for God to send someone else. After

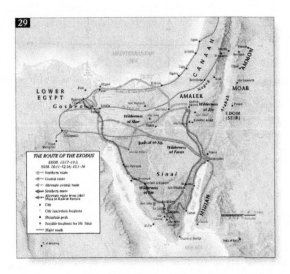

Figure 6 - Briscoe, Thomas V. 1998. Nashville, TN: Holman Bible Atlas, p.66

all, Moses had forgotten much of the Egyptian language after spending forty years in the back desert, herding sheep. He was a different man at the age of 80. He was no longer so sure of himself. No longer was Moses the handsome young Prince of Egypt. He was a Senior Citizen who basically wanted to be left alone. His smooth, clean skin had now aged, with help from the heat and the winds of the desert. The once so defined muscles and smooth skin moved to the southern part of his body and was now replaced with wrinkles and grey hair. His earlier strong, erect body was weaker and more bent over when he walked. And now God called him to this Herculean task? It didn't make sense. God must have made a mistake.

But God doesn't make mistakes. It does seem strange that God often meets us at our weakest point and challenges us with some of our greatest challenges in life. We expect God to use us when we are *"somebody"* in the eyes of many or when we have our health, wealth, position, strength, etc. But often at those times in our lives we are too full of ourselves for Him to operate through us. It's often after we lose what we had and find ourselves needy that He comes to the rescue and says, *"Now I can use you"*. God is in the business of using a *"nobody"* so He can make a *"somebody"* out of them. But because so many people, who believe they are a *"somebody"*, are just too independent with no sense of need, God passes them by until that somebody becomes a nobody. Then they are ready to be used by God.

The Exodus – Motivated By Love

Whether we are in a movie theater, a schoolroom, an office, or any other public place, we are surrounded with *"Exit"* signs. We are aware that the sign is showing us the way out of the room or building in which we are occupied. Likewise, when we speak of the *"Exodus"*, we are referring to the Israelites *"exiting"* the Land of Egypt. Why did God remove the Israelites from Egyptian bondage? Moses gives us this answer when he told his people, *"Because he loved your forefathers and chose their descendants after them, he brought you out of Egypt by his Presence and his great strength, to drive out before you nations greater and stronger than you and to bring you into their land to give it to you for your inheritance, as it is today."* (Deuteronomy 4:37-38) How did Moses remove the people from Egypt? They had been enslaved for 430 years and had been the work-force of Pharaoh.

Honestly, he didn't remove them. God exited them out of Egypt and used Moses as His instrument to bring judgment on an unrepentant Pharaoh. God gave Aaron, Moses' brother, to him as the spokesman to Pharaoh and empowered his staff as an instrument to bring about ten plagues upon the Egyptians. He even told Moses ahead of time that the Pharaoh would not listen to him and would harden his heart to the point that God would have to show

Pharaoh and all Egypt that the God who created the heavens and the earth ruled over nature.

Whereas Pharaoh thought his encounter was with Moses, Moses recognized that Pharaoh's encounter was with the God of all creation, including nature. And so, over a period of weeks and perhaps months, God brought one plague after another upon the Egyptians and their gods: (1) the plague of blood; (2) the plague of frogs; (3) the plague of gnats; (4) the plague of flies; (5) the plague on livestock; (6) the plague of boils; (7) the plague of hail; (8) the plague of locusts; (9) the plague of darkness; and finally (10) the plague of death of the firstborn (Exodus 7:14-11).

The Passover

Pharaoh rejected warning after warning. He ignored the God of all creation by ignoring God's spokesman, Moses. Now the time had come for the deliverance of God's people from bondage and the fulfillment of the promise that God made to Abraham centuries before when He told that great patriarch, *"Know for certain that your descendants will be strangers in a country not their own, and they will be enslaved and mistreated four hundred years. But I will punish the nation they serve as slaves, and afterward they will come out with great possessions"* (Genesis 15:13-14). It was time for God to pronounce the benediction by informing Moses that He was going to institute a new calendar year for His people, along with a wonderful new feast that His people would celebrate for centuries to follow.

"This month is to be for you the first month, the first month of your year" (Exodus 12:2). The new month was known as Nisan or Abib and corresponds to our March-April. On the tenth day of that new month the heads of the Israelite families were to select a

lamb for their family. The lambs were to be year-old males without defect and could be selected from either the sheep or the goats. Then on the fourteenth day of that month they were to slaughter the lamb or goat at twilight. God continued to unveil His plan to Moses by saying, *"Then they are to take some of the blood and put it on the sides and tops of the doorframes of the houses where they eat the lambs"* (Exodus 12:7). God then told Moses, *"On that same night I will pass through Egypt and strike down every first-born – both men and animals – and I will bring judgment on all the gods of Egypt. I am the Lord. The blood will be a sign for you on the houses where you are; and when I see the blood,* **I will pass over you.** *No destructive plague will touch you when I strike Egypt"* (Exodus 12:12-13).

For the people to remember this great night of deliverance, God established a "celebration feast" for them. He told them to *"Celebrate the Feast of Unleavened Bread, because it was on this very day that I brought your divisions out of Egypt. Celebrate this day as a lasting ordinance for the generations to come"* (Exodus 12:17).

But as with the Abrahamic Covenant, there was more. I mean one more promise that God had made to Abraham centuries before this evening. He told Abraham that his descendants would leave the country with wealth they had never experienced as slaves. Was that fulfilled just as God promised? Indeed, it was. God's promise was fulfilled to the letter – *"The Egyptians urged the people to hurry and leave the country . . . The Israelites did as Moses instructed and asked the Egyptians for articles of silver and gold and for clothing. The Lord had made the Egyptians favorably disposed toward the people and they gave them what they asked for, so they plundered the Egyptians"* (Exodus 12:33,35-36). Is that the end of the story? Not at all.

No sooner had the people left Egypt when Pharaoh, who had just lost his firstborn son, changed his mind and pursued the Israelites. The newly released Israelites soon heard the rumble of chariots and the sound of horses' hooves gaining ground behind them. Panic overcame these freed slaves when they found themselves boxed in with the Red Sea in front of them and the Egyptian Army behind them. Once again their faith was tested. Did God still love them? Would He show them His love by somehow protecting them from the swords of the Egyptians? They cried out to Moses for help and once again gazed upon God's love through the raising of a stick.

As Moses raised his staff over the Red Sea, it immediately parted. No one had ever seen such a sight. How could water separate like that? When had such a thing ever happened before? These questions may have entered the minds of the people, but they weren't going to take the time to research any previous unexplained phenomenon. The two and a half million people immediately began to cross through the parted waters, racing as fast as their feet and carts could carry them. When the last person lifted his foot out of the Sea, God closed the waters on the Egyptian Army.

Moses led his people to the place God promised Abraham - Mt. Sinai, where he received the Ten Commandments from God, as well as many other laws and regulations for his people. From this point on, Moses spent forty years with his people, putting up with their complaints and rebellion. You would think that now the people fully recognized God was in charge and He would indeed provide for their needs. Despite God's great deliverance of His people out of Egyptian bondage, the people rebelled again and again.

On one such occasion, Moses was so exasperated by some of the leaders that he took matters into his own hands, just as he had done when he killed an Egyptian. During Moses' forty-year journey through the wilderness, leading this unthankful group and putting up with their nonsense. God told him to speak to a rock. He promised Moses that He would bring water out of the rock for His people. But when Moses stood before the rock, he told his people, *"Listen, you rebels, must we bring you water out of this rock?' 'Then Moses raised his arm and struck the rock twice with his staff. Water gushed out, and the community and their livestock drank'"* (Numbers 20:10-11). *What was wrong with that? Here's God's answer – "But the Lord said to Moses and Aaron, 'Because you did not trust in me enough to honor me as holy in the sight of the Israelites, you will not bring this community into the land I give them'"* (Numbers 20:12).

Moses had communicated to his people that he and Aaron were the ones with the power to bring water from the rock. From God's perspective, it was obviously time for Moses to complete his task of deliverance and turn over the responsibility of taking Israel into the Promised Land to someone else. This meant that someone else would have to lead the people across the Jordan and into the Land of Promise. *"So the Lord said to Moses, 'Take Joshua son of Nun, a man in whom is the spirit, and lay your hand on him. Have him stand before Eleazar the priest and the entire assembly and commission him in their presence. Give him some of your authority so the whole Israelite community will obey him.'"* (Numbers 27:18).

Soon after this event Aaron died on Mount Hor, Moses completed his writings, commissioned Joshua to take the people into the Land and then died on Mt. Nebo. So now we leave the Beginnings of the Nation of Israel and move on to the Settlement of the people into the Land that God promised them since the days of His promise to Abraham. But before we move on, let's reflect on the Passover and its meaning for us today.

REFLECTION - This Passover is an excellent illustration of our own deliverance from the bondage of sin. In fact, Jesus is called our *"Passover Lamb"* – *"For Christ, our Passover lamb, has been sacrificed"* (1Corinthians 5:7b). Jesus rode into Jerusalem on the 10th of Nisan and on the 14th day of Nisan, as the Jews were slaughtering their lambs and goats for Passover, He was nailed to the cross, experienced the slow process of death and finally cried out, *"It is finished"* (John 19:30). The temple curtain was torn in two from top to bottom, darkness covered the sky and even one of the soldiers who pounded nails into our Savior's hands and feet confessed, *"Surely he was the Son of God!"* (Matthew 27:54). This payment for sin was another expression of God's love for mankind. It provided for the penalty of our sin to appease the justice of a holy God who declared through the Apostle Paul that *"the wages of sin is death"* (Romans 6:23) and through the writer to the Hebrews, *"In fact, the law requires that nearly everything be cleansed with blood, and without the shedding of blood there is no forgiveness"* (Hebrews 9:22).

5

Love in a Promise Fulfilled

The Book of Deuteronomy ends with the death of Moses, but God's Story continues. Both Moses and Aaron are dead. The original intent was for the two of them to take the Israelites into the land of Promise. However, due to their own rebellion and dishonoring God, they died with the rest of that first generation; Aaron on Mt. Hor and Moses on Mt. Nebo. However, the purpose of God continued. God chose Joshua to take the place of Moses. He and Caleb were the only men from the first generation that entered the Land because they remained faithful to God. And so, we read in the Book of Joshua, *"After the death of Moses the servant of the Lord, the Lord said to Joshua..."*. (Joshua 1:1).

JOSHUA - He was a military man who knew how to strategize and win battles. When the Israelites arrived outside of the Canaanite city of Jericho, Joshua sent two spies into the city and he learned that the people in the city were terrified of the God of Israel. God then unleashed His new plan to Joshua, telling him to prepare the people and have them consecrate themselves so they could cross the Jordan River the next day. However, the Jordan was at flood stage, which meant that it could be as wide as a mile across. Furthermore, there was no Moses to part the Jordan as he parted the Red Sea. But again, it is God who is leading them, so the problem was God's problem and not man's.

God gave His solution to Joshua, who told his people, *"Now then, choose twelve men from the tribes of Israel, one from each tribe. And as soon as the priests who carry the ark of the Lord – the Lord of all the earth – set foot in the Jordan, its waters flowing downstream will be cut off and stand up in a heap"* (Joshua 3:13). In the process, the Israelites observed that God can choose any man or method to accomplish His purpose. The key qualification was not name recognition, but rather obedience to God and His plan. The people followed Joshua's instructions and crossed the Jordan.

When the last man of that second generation took his feet out of the water, the priests made their way to the bank of the Jordan, stepped out of the river and watched the waters fill the cavity that God had opened for them. They camped at Gilgal, a few miles from Jericho. Then Joshua had every male circumcised, per God's Covenant with Abraham, and celebrated the Passover. That very day the manna (food which God provided in the 40 years of wilderness wandering) stopped and the people began eating the produce of the Land.

Israel was now in the Land of Promise, but so were the Canaanites, whom God wanted to destroy for their sinful practices. Therefore, the Lord gave Joshua a strategy for taking Jericho. Though it was a very strange strategy, it worked. The people marched around the city once a day for six days. On the seventh day, they marched around it seven times, with the priests blowing trumpets. On the seventh walk around, the priests sounded a long blast of the trumpets and the people shouted. The city walls collapsed outward and the Israelites gained a great victory.

PROBLEM - However, the thrill of victory is often followed by the agony of defeat. The next day the people went up the hill to fight those living in Ai. You would think that would be easy compared to the victory over Jericho, but rather than another thrill of victory, the Israelites experienced their first taste of defeat. The people of Ai came out of the city and killed thirty-six Israelites, as they chased them from the city gate as far as the stone quarries and struck them down on the slopes (Joshua 7:4-5). The people were now terrified to move on. What could have gone wrong? As Joshua cried out to God, the Lord told him that there was sin in the camp. Someone had taken that which belonged to God.

Before the victory over Jericho, the Lord told them plainly that the things of Jericho belonged to Him. It was the principle of the "first fruits". The first of the harvest belonged to God. Jericho was the first of many cities in the Land. The Israelites were permitted to take anything after that for themselves, but the first fruits belonged to God and someone had taken some of that for himself. Through a very specific process of discovery, Achan was found to be the culprit. He confessed what he had done by saying, **"I SAW, I COVETED, I TOOK and I HID"** (Joshua 7:20-21).

Eve followed the same line of sin. She **SAW** that the fruit was good. She **COVETED** the fruit. She **TOOK** a bite of the fruit and gave it to Adam so that he also would eat. The result? They **HID** from God (Genesis 3:6).

King David followed the same pattern. He **SAW** Bathsheba bathing out on her roof. He **COVETED** another man's wife. He **TOOK** another man's wife into his bedroom and committed adultery with her. Then he attempted to **HIDE** what he had done by trying to get her husband to sleep with her. When Uriah refused to sleep with his wife, David had him placed in the fiercest part of the battle to be killed (2Samuel 11).

Even the Apostle John addressed this process in his first Epistle when he wrote, *"For everything in the world – the cravings of sinful man, the lust of his eyes and the boasting of what he has and does – comes not from the Father but from the world"* (1John 2:16).

Most of our temptations come from what we **see**. We see something that we want. The more we think about it, the more we want it. After a while it becomes an **obsession** and we feel that we must have it, whether it is profitable or harmful. We justify our **taking** what may belong to someone else by thinking, *"I deserve this"*. And then when we are caught, we do everything in our power to **"hide"** the fact of what we've done. We may deny it, blame someone else or excuse our actions by saying that everyone else does it.

Once Joshua took care of the problem, Israel left Jericho and defeated Ai, using an entirely different strategy than what they used in Jericho. From Ai Joshua led his people and proceeded up to an old city named Shechem (present day Nablus). It's nestled between two mountains: Mount Gerizim and Mt. Ebal. Why did they go there? They were carrying out Moses' orders when he told them to renew the Covenant in the new Land. Moses gave this directive, *"When the Lord your God has brought you into the land you are entering to possess, you are to proclaim on Mount Gerizim the blessings, and on Mount Ebal the curses"* (Deuteronomy 11:29). Then Joshua took his people to that area in obedience to Moses' command.

From this point on Joshua took the Central area of the country, then the Southern area and finally the Northern area. It took about seven years to conquer the land that God had given to them. Joshua then divided the Land among the twelve tribes. All but one of the tribes were satisfied with their inheritance. However, the tribe of Dan decided to leave the coastal area they had been given and took the northern most part of the Promised Land, near Mt. Hermon.

Though Israel finally settled down in the Land, they did not fully drive out the people. This became a stumbling block due to intermarriage and led to idolatry and a series of judgments from God.

Spiritual & Moral Collapse – The Time Of The Judges

The Israelites fell into idolatry again and again as they intermarried with the Canaanites and adopted their worship and their gods. The Lord would then raise up one of the nearby nations to destroy their crops and enslave some of the people from time to time. When Israel cried out to God in repentance, He raised up warriors, whom the people called judges. This warrior would deliver God's people from their enemies and the people would once again worship the Lord. But for several hundred years, this cycle was repeated and became known as the time of the Judges. And it is during this same time frame that a Moabite woman, fell in love with a Jewish man who emerged on the scene. The woman's name was Ruth and the Jewish man's name was Boaz. You'll have to read the Book of Ruth to get the details, but it is a fascinating love story that you won't want to miss.

As time progressed, God raised up a man as the bridge between the times of the Judges and the time of the Kings. In fact, he is the last of the judges and the first of the prophets. This man Samuel also had the opportunity to anoint the first King of Israel.

SAMUEL – Samuel has an interesting history. His mother Elizabeth was barren for many years. As the years passed, the hope for a child seemed more distant than ever. However, Elizabeth was a woman of faith, so she decided to bring the matter before the Lord once again. But this time, she added a promise - she would give back her child to the Lord after he was weaned. God answered her prayer and Elizabeth fulfilled her promise to the Lord.

Young Samuel was brought up in Shiloh, the place where the Tabernacle was being kept, along with the Ark of the Covenant. His mentor was Eli the priest. After Eli's death, the people turned to Samuel and saw him as their prophet. Samuel prophesied for many years, the same time that the prophet Elijah and later, the prophet Elisha, ministered to the people of Israel, challenging them to return to the Lord. As time passed and the end of Samuel's time as prophet was fast approaching, Samuel expected his sons to inherit his role. However, the people rejected his sons because they were corrupt. In place of Eli's sons, the people demanded a king. God told Samuel to give them their request and anoint Saul to become the first King of Israel.

As we continue our acronym, My BaSKET, we will now look at the K.

K is for the **Kingdom** of Israel. Though God was their actual King, the people wanted to be like the nations around them and have a physical, human king with whom they could identify. The prophet **Samuel** was convinced that the people were rejecting him, but God told him to go ahead and appoint a king for the people because they were not against Samuel. They were rejecting God's rule over them. As the last of the judges and the first of the prophets, Samuel bridged the period from Settlement to Kingdom by appointing Israel's first King.

KING SAUL – I call him the Reluctant King because he never wanted to be king. In fact, he ran and hid from those who tried to persuade him to take the role. Saul finally agreed to the task and started his kingship on a good note. But in a short time, King Saul was more fearful of the people than He was of God. He disobeyed God on two occasions, so God told Samuel to inform King Saul that He would remove Saul's position and give it to someone more worthy of that title and position – a man after God's own heart. However, the exchange did not take place overnight. In fact, years passed as a young musician was brought into Saul's palace to play the harp when an evil spirit troubled King Saul. That young man was loved by King Saul and eventually became a young warrior in Saul's army. This young David moved up the corporate ladder from the life of a shepherd to a musician in Saul's palace to a gutsy warrior who was willing to go face to face with a giant of a man named Goliath. After David's victorious battle over Goliath, Saul immediately enlisted him in his army and gave David his daughter in marriage.

For a while things went well until one day after a battle, Saul and his entourage marched back to the city. The women came out dancing and singing, as they always did after a battle that led to victory. Only this time their words pierced the very soul of King Saul. They sang, *"Saul has slain his thousands, and David his tens of thousands"* (1Samuel 18:7). Immediately Saul became furiously jealous and was afraid of David. From that point on, King Saul determined to get rid of this young warrior once and for all.

During the pursuing years, King Saul did everything he could to kill David, but the young man was under God's protection. Then it happened. King Saul and his army fought against the Philistines on Mount Gilboa. Someone in the Philistine army shot an arrow King Saul's way and pierced the heart of the King. Saul realized that the end was near, but he was still alive. He didn't want to be captured alive by the Philistines so he fell on his sword and died. When the enemy saw the body of the king lying still, they cut off his head and dragged his body to the top of Beth Shan, where they impaled him on the wall of the city.

When David heard about the King's death, he didn't rejoice. No, he mourned for his king because he knew that King Saul was the anointed of God. But it soon became obvious that Israel needed a King and eventually David was given that honor in Hebron, a city south of Jerusalem. Eventually all of Israel wanted David to rule over them, so David conquered the Jebusite city of Jebus and renamed it the City of David.

KING DAVID – What can we say about this multi-talented young king? He excelled as a warrior, had the skill of a harpist, wrote music, designed instruments for worship, and possessed the gift of a poet and a heart for God. At the same time, David also had a passion for women. Most often that mixture can get any man into a lot of trouble and David was no exception.

In many ways David was a complex man. He loved and worshipped the Lord and penned half of the Psalms in Scripture. He was a man of deep prayer and wanted the nations to recognize the God of all creation. And yet one woman was not enough for David. He violated his loyalty to one of his mighty men by taking that man's wife for himself and then had the Captain of the Army place the woman's husband at the front lines, withdraw the troops from him and allow the enemy to kill him. But when confronted with his sin by Nathan the prophet, David immediately repented and God forgave him. But David paid a steep price for that sin. The new born child of David and Bathsheba died. His entire family was in disarray. One son killed another son for violating his sister. A third son attempted a coup over his father's kingdom and almost succeeded before he was killed. And though David had promised the Kingdom to his son Solomon, another son just about stole the kingdom from this appointed heir until David got wind of the plot. David immediately secured the throne for his son Solomon.

KING SOLOMON – Solomon also enjoyed writing and we can thank him for some of the Psalms, The Song of Solomon, The Book of Proverbs and The Book of Ecclesiastes. His writings reveal the development of his mind and soul, as well as his sad drift away from God.

Solomon began his reign in such a godly way by carrying out the vision of his father David and building a great and marvelous Temple for the Lord. This young king then dedicated it with a masterful prayer. When he finished his prayer of dedication, the glory of the Lord filled the Temple. What a beginning!

However, Solomon also had a passion for women and began selecting the women from the people of other nations who worshipped other gods. This was a direct violation of God's command; *"You must not intermarry with them, because they will surely turn your hearts after their gods"* (1Kings 11:2). The Bible tells us the result of this proliferation of wives – *"As Solomon grew old, his wives turned his heart after other gods, and his heart was not fully devoted to the Lord his God, as the heart of David his father had been"* (1Kings 11:4).

As Solomon aged and eventually was approaching the end of his life, he wrote the Book of Ecclesiastes. One of the habits senior citizens have is reflecting over their years. They begin to repeat statements to themselves like *"What if"*, *"if only,"* *"I remember when I used to. . ."*. As Solomon thought about his forty-year reign, he questioned what all his fame, money, building accomplishments and wisdom had done for him. How did he handle the gifts of wisdom, money, knowledge and fame? Not very well.

He had many regrets and concluded that all of what he possessed and accomplished wasn't worth it. Here are some of his conclusions: (1) wisdom is meaningless; (2) pleasures are meaningless; (3) folly is meaningless; (4) toil is meaningless; (5) advancement is meaningless; (6) riches are meaningless. Then he concludes with these words, *"Now all has been heard; here is the conclusion of the matter: Fear God and keep his commandments, for this is the whole duty of man. For God will bring every deed into judgment, including every hidden thing whether it is good or evil"* (Ecclesiastes 12:13-14).

And there is one more statement Solomon made a little earlier in his writing this Book. He knew that he wouldn't be around forever and so he tried to envision who would inherit all that he dreamed about and built to perfection. Here was Solomon's concern; *"I hated all the things I had toiled for under the sun, because I must leave them to the one who comes after me. And who knows whether he will be a wise man or a fool? Yet he will have control over all the work into which I have poured my effort and skill under the sun"* (Ecclesiastes 2:18-19).

Let's think about that. We build up all types of equity in our lives including money, property, various possessions, reputation and character. What is the most important part of our equity that we want to leave to our family? Too much money can result in a lot of problems if they are not trained on how to handle money properly. The same is true with our property and possessions. That could result in an abundance for the kids to fight over. Then there's our reputation, which may or may not match our character. Our friends and associates may know us by our reputation, but how well do they know our character, which has never been hidden from our kids who know both and may have seen a contrast? Had Solomon spent more time developing his own character, he would have left a much better inheritance to the one son who followed him into the Kingdom.

Remember Solomon's concern over who would inherit everything that he spent his life creating and developing? He was concerned whether he would leave his inheritance to a wise man or a fool. We don't have to read very far to find the answer to that question.

The Divided Kingdom

There are many business owners who have built up a great business, along with a great reputation, only to be torn down by a lazy or incompetent son. Likewise, great corporations are established by visionaries and pioneers who are willing to pay the price of 16-hour days, sleepless nights balancing the budget, experiencing huge losses and even bankruptcy, only to rebuild and regain a great business and reputation once again. But then a son or grandson comes along and within a matter of years, he runs that once magnificent corporation into the ground. Employees are released in the process, bills remain unpaid, quality of work deteriorates and eventually the entire business fails.

The United Kingdom was something like a magnificent corporation that lasted 120 years. But when Solomon's son, Rehoboam came to power, he decided to be harsher on the people than his father had been. He rejected the wise counsel of Solomon's counselors and bought into the foolish counsel of his close, young friends. This resulted in a split between the Northern tribes and the Southern tribes. Rehoboam lost ten of the tribes to the Northern part of Israel, which became known as Israel. He ended up with two and a half tribes in the South known as Judah.

Figure 8 – Dr. Yohn Teaching at the city of
DAN. Photo taken by Jason Elam

There were no good kings in Israel because they immediately went into idolatry when their first King, Jeroboam set up two golden calves and placed one in the city of Dan (The northern most city in Israel) and the other in the city of Bethel (The southernmost city in Israel). The photo shows me teaching in front of the duplicate altar where Jeroboam set up his golden calf in the city of Dan. Jeroboam developed this plan to keep his people from returning to Jerusalem, telling his people that they did not have to weary themselves and travel the whole way to Jerusalem to worship God. Instead, they could go either to Dan or Bethel and accomplish the same thing by worshiping one of the golden calves. This Divided Kingdom lasted for 345 years, from 931 B.C. to 586 B.C.

The first Kingdom to reject God's love and taste His fury was Israel, the Northern Kingdom. At the time, this Kingdom was under the Kingship of Hoshea who depended upon Egypt for his security rather than God. In 722 B.C. God brought the Assyrians down from the North and removed the Israelites from their homeland and deported them throughout the Mesopotamia area. Then he replenished the former Kingdom with Gentiles from Mesopotamia so that the northern region became known as "Galilee of The Gentiles" (Isaiah 9:1-2).

We would think that her sister nation of Judah would immediately repent of their sins and turn to God, when they saw what happened to Israel. But rather than repent of their own sins, that nation followed the evil ways of their sister nation Israel and worshipped many other gods. Because of Judah's rebellion and idolatry, the Lord brought the King of Babylon against them on three different occasions. The Babylonians first invaded the Land of Judah in 605 B.C. and removed several people from that region, including Daniel the prophet. Then in 597 B.C. King Nebuchadnezzar once again invaded Judah and this time removed the Prophet Ezekiel from the Land and brought him to Babylon. Finally, in 586 B.C. King Nebuchadnezzar invaded the land, the City of Jerusalem and destroyed everything in sight, including the beautiful Temple of Solomon that he had personally dedicated to Jehovah. This brought an end to the Kingdom Period of Israel.

In the next chapter, you will learn about the books that cover this period, and then in chapter seven, we'll begin our journey into the Exile and Triumphal Return Period by discovering a unique man of God who refused to compromise, even when his life depended on it. His name is Daniel. We know him as the Prophet Daniel who wrote the words of the Book named after him.

Because of Judah's persistent rebellion against God by serving other gods, the Lord fulfilled His promise of the curse and brought the nation of Babylon against them to remove them from the Land for 70 years.

Besides the fact that God sent prophet after prophet to warn His people about His discipline for worshipping other gods, He gave them the Torah, the first five books of the Bible. Listen to what the Lord included in these writings of Moses: *"However, if you do not obey the Lord your God and do not carefully follow all his commands and decrees I am giving you today, all these curses will come upon you and overtake you: You will be cursed in the city and cursed in the country. Your basket and your kneading trough will be cursed . . .The Lord will cause you to be defeated before your enemies. . . The alien who lives among you will rise above you higher and higher, but you will sink lower and lower . . . The Lord will bring a nation against you from far away, from the ends of the earth, like an eagle swooping down, a nation whose language you will not understand, a fierce-looking nation without respect for the old or pity for the young. . ."* (Deuteronomy 28:15-17;25; 43; 40-50).

Let's quickly review the last chapter. God raised up a great Kingdom under the Kingships of Saul, David and Solomon. But Solomon's son Rehoboam lost ten of the twelve tribes to the Northern Kingdom of Israel. But due to the rebellion of Israel and then Judah, God did exactly what He had promised to do.

There are other stories of God's love through this tumultuous period, but I will share just a few of them. God often raised up prophets, not only to declare His message to others, but also to live His message for other eyes to observe. Two prophets that come to mind are Ezekiel and Hosea. As Ezekiel faithfully prophesied to his people, the Lord told him that it would cost him the life of his wife – *"The word of the Lord came to me: 'Son of man, with one blow I am about to take away from you the delight of your eyes. Yet do not lament or weep or shed any tears. Groan quietly; do not mourn for the dead. Keep your turban fastened and your sandals on your feet; do not cover the lower part of your face or eat the customary food of mourners." 'So I spoke to the people in the morning, and in the evening my wife died. The next morning, I did as I had been commanded'"* (Ezekiel 24:15-18)

Hosea, on the other hand, did not lose his wife to death, but lost her to prostitution. It's one thing for a man to choose his wife and later discover her unfaithfulness, but quite another when you are told to marry an unfaithful wife at the very outset. Again, listen to God's directive to this prophet, *"Go, take to yourself an adulterous wife and children of unfaithfulness, because the land is guilty of the vilest adultery in departing from the Lord"* (Hosea 1:2). The prophet obeyed, fathered two children with her, and then watched her leave him for other lovers.

God came to the prophet again and told him, *"Go, show your love to your wife again, though she is loved by another and is an adulteress. Love her as the Lord loves the Israelites, though they turn to other gods and love the sacred raisin cakes"* (Hosea 3:1). In obedience to the Lord, Hosea buys her back from her lover and loves her once again.

However, the northern kingdom of Israel continued in her adulterous ways and finally experienced the sword of the Assyrian in 722 B.C., who removed her from her once lofty position, took her back to Assyria, and repopulated that once robust kingdom with Gentiles.

Hosea's wife, Gomer, was an illustration of the northern kingdom of Israel. Though God saw Israel as His "wife" and was faithful to her, she left Him and pursued other lovers. However, God was always there calling her back to Himself.

Sadly, Gomer also represents us for though God has always been faithful to us, we too often prostitute ourselves with other lovers, leaving Him behind. But remember, the entire Bible is God's love story for us to realize that He continues to wait for us to return to Him. He promises to forgive us for our waywardness, attitude, and behavior. He cries out to us, *"Here am I, here am I!"*

ISAIAH – *"The Prince of the Prophets"* (740-690 B.C.)

The Book of Isaiah is often considered to be a microcosm of the entire Bible. Just as there are 66 books in the Bible, so are there 66 chapters in the Book of Isaiah. This prophet prophesied for a long period during the reigns of Uzziah, Jotham, Ahaz, and Hezekiah, kings of Judah. Isaiah's ministry lasted about fifty years.

At the time of his prophecy, the Northern Kingdom had approximately twenty years left before the Assyrians would come down and invade it, removing its occupants and repopulating it with Gentiles. That judgment on the Northern Kingdom should have been a warning and object lesson to Judah, the Southern Kingdom. However, they did not learn from God's judgment on Israel. The people of Judah continued to be religious, but their hearts were elsewhere. God condemned them saying, *"Stop bringing meaningless offerings! Your incense is detestable to me . . . When you spread out your hands in prayer, I will hide my eyes from you; even if you offer many prayers, I will not listen."* (Isaiah 1:13,15).

But after this powerful rebuke, God still loves the people and wants them to return to Him. So, He pleads with them, *"Come now, let us reason together,' says the Lord. 'Though your sins are like scarlet, they shall be as white as snow; though they are red as crimson, they shall be like wool'"* (Isaiah 1:18).

You can divide this Book into two sections. The first part includes Isaiah 1-39 and is a message of coming judgment on Judah. But beginning with the next chapter, Isaiah provides a beautiful message of hope and restoration in chapters 40-66.

Perhaps one of the most compelling chapters in this Book is Isaiah 53. It is the perfect description of a suffering Messiah. And though many rabbis interpret the passage as referring to the nation of Israel, it is evident to anyone who reads it that Isaiah is speaking about a future Messiah, fulfilled in the man from Nazareth named Jesus. Consider just a few of the verses from this passage:

"But he was pierced for our transgressions, he was crushed for our iniquities; the punishment that brought us peace was upon him, and by his wounds we are healed. We all, like sheep, have gone astray, each of us has turned to his own way; and the Lord has laid on him the iniquity of us all . . . For he bore the sin of many, and made intercession for the transgressors" (Isaiah 53:5,6,12). After reading these verses, turn to the four crucifixion scenes in the four Gospels – Matthew 27:32-56; Mark 15:21-41; Luke 23:33-43; and John 19:17-37.

In fact, the other day I was reading 1 Peter and came across a few verses that I thought sounded quite familiar and soon realized Peter was reflecting on Isaiah's prophecy and paraphrased some passages in Isaiah 53. Listen to the following passages from Peter – *"He committed no sin, and no deceit was found in his mouth. When they hurled their insults at him, he did not retaliate: when he suffered, he made no threats. Instead he entrusted himself to him who judges justly. He himself bore our sins in his body on the tree, so that we might die to sins and live for righteousness: by his wounds you have been healed. For you were like sheep going astray, but now you have returned to the Shepherd and Overseer of your souls"* (1 Peter 2:22-25). Now compare Peter's comments with Isaiah 53:5-8,12.

Though the people of Judah had gone the way of the northern kingdom of Israel, God continued to demonstrate His love for them by crying out, *"Here am I, here am I. all day long I have held out my hands to an obstinate people who walk in ways not good, pursuing their own imaginations . . ."* (Isaiah 65:2).

God sent many other prophets to His people during the Kingdom Period, but both Israel and Judah decided they knew better than God and carved out a lifestyle they preferred. And as a man sows what he reaps, so does a nation. In 586 B.C. God brought the Babylonians to Jerusalem to destroy the city that bore His Name.

There are other prophets and other Books in the Old Testament that contribute to this love story from God, but to maintain our focus on God's love, we will move to the Time of Judah's Exile in Babylon.

6

Love Through Discipline & Mercy

U p to this point, we've learned the acronym, My BaSKET, as Mankind, Beginnings, Settlement, and Kingdom. Now we will look at the "E".

E stands for **Exile.**

Within 136 years of when the Assyrians removed the people of Israel from the Northern Kingdom, the Southern Kingdom of Judah followed suit and went into idolatry. Though there were eight kings in the Southern Kingdom who followed God, the people themselves followed other gods, so the Lord raised up the Babylonians to come down and remove the people of Judah to Babylon for a 70-year period.

The first invasion occurred in 605 B.C. when a young man named Daniel was taken out of Jerusalem to Babylon. A second invasion took place in 597 B.C. and another young man named Ezekiel was removed from Jerusalem and taken to Babylon. Then the final invasion came when Nebuchadnezzar, king of Babylon, destroyed the temple of Solomon and the city of Jerusalem in 586

B.C. During that seventy-year period, both Daniel and Ezekiel became prophets who preached to both the captives in Babylon as well as the remnant of Jews in Jerusalem.

We may wonder how God was showing love when He raised up the Babylonians and brought them to Jerusalem. Where was His love when the Babylonians destroyed the City in which God had placed His Name and the Temple that allowed people to worship their God? The answer to this question is found in a New Testament passage where the Writer of Hebrews quotes from an Old Testament passage that reads, *"My son, do not make light of the Lord's discipline, and do not lose heart when he rebukes you, because the Lord disciplines those he loves, and he punishes everyone he accepts as a son"*[1]. Just as we discipline our children because we want them to learn not to do certain things, as well as what they should be doing, so does God discipline us because of His love for us.

God never stopped loving His people Israel, though they rejected Him. He wanted them to learn that He alone was their Provider and Protector. When they were despised by the nations of the world, He wanted them to realize that He still loved them and was disciplining them because of His love. And though not all the people recognized His love through discipline, three individuals did. They honored and worshipped Him while in captivity. We begin with the young man Daniel who was removed from everything familiar in the first Babylonian invasion. Let me now introduce you to a man who never compromised his principles nor his character.

DANIEL in Babylon – God was not only disciplining His own people, but He also used some of them to make known His

---

1. Hebrews 12:5-6 quoted from Proverbs 3:11-12

love to other nations. Yes, Nebuchadnezzar, King of Babylon, was a cruel man who was convinced that he alone was responsible for the victories he experienced on the battlefield. And God alone had the power to change His mind by raising up Daniel in the King's palace.

Though he was just one of many captives in Babylon, Daniel had a major impact on the Babylonian King Nebuchadnezzar. One evening Nebuchadnezzar dreamed of a great metallic statue, whose head was made of gold, its chest and arms of silver, its belly and thighs of bronze, its legs of iron, and its feet partly of iron and partly of baked clay. Daniel said that King Nebuchadnezzar was the head of gold. After him will come three other kingdoms, which in Scripture and history were Medo-Persia, Greece and Rome.

The King was so impressed with Daniel's ability to interpret dreams that he put him in charge of all the wise men and ruler over the entire province of Babylon. Furthermore, Daniel's three friends became administrators over the province of Babylon, while Daniel remained at the royal court.

Later, Daniel warned the king to *"Renounce your sins by doing what is right, and your wickedness by being kind to the oppressed. . ."* (Daniel 4:27). The King refused to listen to Daniel's advice, went raving mad and lived like a wild animal for seven years. He finally came to his senses and acknowledged the God of heaven when he confessed, *"I, Nebuchadnezzar, raised my eyes toward heaven, and my sanity was restored. Then I praised the Most High. I honored and glorified him who lives forever. His dominion is an eternal dominion; his kingdom endures from generation to generation. All the peoples of the earth are regarded as nothing. He does as he pleases with the powers of heaven and the peoples of the earth. No one can hold back his hand or say to him: 'What have you done?'"* (Daniel 4:34-36).

EZEKIEL in Babylon - During the same time, the Prophet Ezekiel was warning the people in Babylon to turn to the Lord. He had been taken to Babylon in 597 B.C. and could see what was about to happen to Jerusalem unless the people repented of their sins. The destruction of Jerusalem was still eleven years away, so there was still time for the people to turn to the Lord. But despite Ezekiel's continuous warnings, those remaining in Jerusalem continued to worship other gods.

In visions, the Holy Spirit took Ezekiel to Jerusalem to see the idolatry of the priests in the Temple. Ezekiel also saw the Glory of the Lord depart from the Temple and move toward the East, down and across the Kidron Valley, and up to the Mount of Olives. Ezekiel writes of the experience – *"The glory of the Lord went up from within the city and stopped above the mountain east of it. The Spirit lifted me up and brought me to the exiles in Babylon in the vision given by the Spirit of God. Then the vision I had seen went up from me, and I told the exiles everything the Lord had shown me"* (Ezekiel 10:23-25). And while Ezekiel was warning his people from Babylon, the Prophet Jeremiah, still living in Jerusalem, continued to call the people to repentance. Those living in Jerusalem refused to listen to Ezekiel, as well as Jeremiah. So, in 586 B.C. the Babylonians destroyed Jerusalem and the Temple.

Once Jerusalem was destroyed, Ezekiel's message changed. He wanted his people in Babylon to know that God was not finished with them. He still loved them and had a plan for them. And just as Ezekiel was given a vision of the departure of God's Glory, so did the Spirit give him a vision of the return of God's Glory – *"Then the man brought me to the gate facing east, and I saw the glory of the God of Israel coming from the east . . . The glory of the Lord entered the temple through the gate facing east.*

Then the Spirit lifted me up and brought me into the inner court, and the glory of the Lord filled the temple. While the man was standing beside me, I heard someone speaking to me from inside the temple. He said: 'Son of man, this is the place of my throne and the place for the soles of my feet. This is where I will live among the Israelites forever. The house of Israel will never again defile my holy name – neither they nor their kings – by their prostitution and the lifeless idols of their kings at their high places" (Ezekiel 43:1-7)

As Ezekiel was attempting to persuade the Jewish captives to turn back to the Lord in Babylon, the Prophet Jeremiah remained in Jerusalem pleading with his people as the destruction of Jerusalem was rapidly closing in on them. But the people continued in their idolatry, burning incense to other gods, and rejecting every love language expression from their God.

JEREMIAH THE PROPHET IN JERUSALEM – Jeremiah was known for preaching gloom and doom because he could see what was about to take place. He pleaded with his people by telling them - *"This whole country will become a desolate wasteland, and these nations will serve the king of Babylon seventy years. But when the seventy years are fulfilled, I will punish the king of Babylon and his nation, the land of the Babylonians, for their guilt, 'declares the Lord, 'and will make it desolate forever'"* (Jeremiah 25:11-12).

The first half of his prophecy focused on the impending destruction of this beloved city of Jerusalem. However, the Lord wanted His people to know that He still loved them and had a future for them, so Jeremiah added the second part of the prophecy providing hope while in captivity. God would deal with their captors. Furthermore, Jeremiah also provided a hope for Israel's return to their land. He promised, *"When seventy years are completed for Babylon, I will come to you and fulfill my gracious promise to bring you back to this place. For I know the plans I have for you' declares the Lord, 'plans to prosper you and not to harm you, plans to give you hope and a future'"* (Jeremiah 29:10-11).

When the prophecy concerning the captivity and destruction of Jerusalem occurred, Jeremiah penned the following words, as a broken-hearted prophet, *"How deserted lies the city, once so full of people! How like a widow is she, who once was great among the nations! She who was queen among the provinces has now become a slave"* (Lamentations 1:1)

ESTHER – Most people know very little about this woman, so I have provided significant detail for how God used her to save countless lives of her people. It's the story of a potential Holocaust in Persia. And God's love permeates through the events of this woman's Cinderella Story.

Her story is one that included a Jewish Uncle, Mordecai, who reared his niece Esther. As she grew into young womanhood, she became a beautiful young woman. Due to a marital dispute between Xerxes, King of Persia and his Queen, the King deposed the Queen and decided to look for a replacement.

It was decided that a contest be held and a search for the most beautiful woman would be made. Various women were groomed to meet the King, and eventually Esther was the chosen one. Mordecai warned her of one specific thing – *"Don't let them know you are a Jew"*. As time passed, her Uncle Mordecai heard about a plot against the King and made it known to Esther, who in turn told the King. The two who plotted against the King were hanged and the incident was recorded in the King's annals.

In the meantime, a man named Haman was a very high official and whenever he went in and out of the palace, everyone would bow. Everyone that is, except Uncle Mordecai. This got under Haman's skin. And when Haman discovered that Mordecai was a Jew, he went to the King and told him, *"There is a certain people dispersed and scattered among the peoples in all the provinces of your kingdom whose customs are different from those of all other people and who do not obey the king's laws; it is not in the king's best interest to tolerate them. If it pleases the king, let a decree be issued to destroy them and I will put ten thousand talents of silver into the royal treasury for the men who carry out this business"* (Esther 3:8-9). In other words, it wouldn't cost the King anything to make such a decree. Without blinking an eye, the King took his signet ring and gave it to Haman. He then said, *"Keep the money and do with the people as you please"* (Esther 3:11).

Can you imagine life under such a rule? The man in charge was too busy or preoccupied to pay much attention to the request. King Xerxes held the power of life and death over all his subjects. And on this occasion, the king possessed an attitude of, "after all, it's just people". What difference does it make if an entire ethnic group disappears? The King had many more subjects in his domain. But little did the king know that he was also sentencing his new bride to her death.

When Uncle Mordecai learned about this decree, he immediately went to Queen Esther and told her, *"Do not think that because you are in the king's house you alone of all the Jews will escape. For if you remain silent at this time, relief and deliverance for the Jews will arise from another place, but you and your father's family will perish. And who knows but that you have come to royal position for such a time as this?"* (Esther 4:12-14). Mordecai raised the issue that perhaps the reason Esther had been chosen to be Queen, was not only the choice of the Persian King, but also the choice of the King of the Universe.

After much prayer, Esther informed the King of Haman's plot. It was also brought to the attention of the King that one of those to be put to death was the man who uncovered a plot against the king and warned him of that plot. The Persian King could not counter his previous decision, but he could add to that decision. He hanged Haman on the gallows that Haman was preparing for Mordecai and then gave Mordecai the position that Haman once enjoyed. He further told the Jews that they could defend themselves.

The Jews were thrilled with the new edict and defended themselves, receiving help from many others. All this took place on the 13th day of the month Adar and on the 14th day they rested and made it a day of feasting and joy. This feast became known as the Feast of Purim, which Jews celebrate even today.

This love story from God continues as we now come to the final Period of the Old Testament history of Israel and our acronym of **My BaSKET** is completed with the "T". We've traced God's love story through Mankind, Beginnings of Israel, Settlement of Israel, the Kingdom of Israel, the Exile of Israel, and now the Triumphal Return of Israel.

T stands for the **Triumphal Return** of the Jews to their homeland. After the 70-year captivity, God moved the heart of Cyrus, the Persian King, who succeeded King Xerxes, to send the Jews back to Jerusalem. The Scriptures record the event – *"In the first year of Cyrus king of Persia, in order to fulfill the word of the Lord spoken by Jeremiah, the Lord moved the heart of Cyrus king of Persia to make a proclamation throughout his realm and to put it in writing: 'This is what Cyrus king of Persia says: 'The Lord, the God of heaven, has given me all the kingdoms of the earth and he has appointed me to build a temple for him at Jerusalem in Judah. Anyone of his people among you – may his God be with him, and let* *him go up to Jerusalem in Judah and build the temple of the Lord, the God of Israel, the God who is in Jerusalem . . . ".* (Ezra 1:1-3 – NIV)

Just as there were three invasions of Jerusalem by Nebuchadnezzar, king of Babylon to deport the Jews, so were there three returns to Jerusalem by the Jews. The first return occurred in 538 B.C. under Zerubbabel, who became the governor of Jerusalem. He took with him approximately 50,000 Jews to build the Temple. It became known as Zerubbabel's Temple. Four hundred years later, King Herod greatly extended the Temple Mount and soon the Temple became known as Herod's Temple. Now let's meet another man of God, Ezra the priest.

EZRA – He knew God's love by personal experience. In 458 B. C. Ezra, the priest returned with a group of Jews to rebuild worship for the Temple. Listen to how the Bible describes this man's credentials – *"this Ezra came up from Babylon. He was a teacher well versed in the Law of Moses, which the Lord, the God of Israel, had given. . . For Ezra had devoted himself to the study and observance of the Law of the Lord, and the teaching its decrees and laws in Israel. . . a man learned in matters concerning the commands and decrees of the Lord for Israel"* (Ezra 7:6,10).

He was both a student and a teacher of God's Word. He was a man who knew the Word, knew what it meant, understood how to interpret life and events around him through the prism of Scripture. And on several occasions, Ezra expressed God's love to His own people after they returned from Babylonian captivity with Zerubbabel, the governor. They laid the foundation for a new Temple and sang with praise and thanksgiving, "He is good; his love to Israel endures forever" (Ezra 3:11). The people came to realize that God had never stopped loving them, even though they had stopped worshipping Him.

On another occasion, Ezra himself spoke about God's love when he wrote, *"Blessed be the Lord, the God of our fathers, who put such a thing as this into the heart of the king, to beautify the house of the Lord that is in Jerusalem, and who extended to me his steadfast love before the king and his counselors, and before all the king's mighty officers. I took courage, for the hand of the Lord my God was on me, and I gathered leading men from Israel to go up with me."* (Ezra 7:27-28 - ESV)

The third time that Ezra spoke about God's love for His people came in the form of a prayer. He first confessed the sin of his people, then recognized the reason why God led them into captivity, but concluded with these words of hope – *"But now for a brief moment favor has been shown by the Lord our God, to leave us a remnant and to give us a secure hold within his holy place, that our God may brighten our eyes and grant us a little reviving in our slavery. For we are slaves. Yet our God has not forsaken us in our slavery, but has extended to us his steadfast love before the kings of Persia, to grant us some reviving to set up the house of our God, to repair its ruins, and to give us protection in Judea and Jerusalem."* (Ezra 9:9 - ESV)

Out of all the Bible characters in Scripture, Ezra would be my choice of a mentor. As a life-long learner, I would love to carry those same credentials. And after studying the Scriptures for over fifty years, I am recognizing more and more just how much I don't know. Ezra, where are you when I need you? Let's now consider a man who had a very high position when he was living in Babylon, but gave it all up to accomplish what only a man of his caliber and disposition could do. His name is Nehemiah.

NEHEMIAH - In 445 B.C. Nehemiah returned to Jerusalem so that he could build the walls of the city. He held a very important position in Persia as the King's Cupbearer. In other words, if someone wanted to poison the king, Nehemiah would be the first to taste the poison.

How did Nehemiah express God's love through Israel's captivity and return to rebuild? When Nehemiah heard about the despair of those who had returned to Jerusalem and that the walls of the city continued to lie in ruins, he called out to God with these words, *"O Lord, God of heaven, the great and awesome God, who keeps his covenant of love with those who love him and obey his commands, let your ear be attentive and your eyes open to hear the prayer your servant is praying before you day and night . . ."* (Nehemiah 1:5-6)

Yes, God had allowed the Babylonians to destroy the city and take Judah, the Southern Kingdom captive. True, they were in bondage for seventy years. But God did not stop loving them, anymore than parents stop loving their children during discipline. The fact that the Jews returned to their homeland was a testimony of God's love for His people.

When Nehemiah entered Jerusalem, he did not let anyone know who he was or why he was there. He spent three days riding around on his horse, surveying the damage. He then called the officials together and said to them, *"You see the trouble we are in: Jerusalem lies in ruins, and its gates have been burned with fire. Come, let us rebuild the wall of Jerusalem and we will no longer be in disgrace"* (Nehemiah 2:17). Nehemiah then informed the people of how God graciously paved the way for him to be in Jerusalem. When they heard that he also had the King's blessing they replied, *"Let us start rebuilding"*(Nehemiah 2:18).

Nehemiah was both an organizer and delegator of responsibility. He came up with an ingenious plan of action by having the people work on the areas of the wall where they lived. This gave them a real incentive to make certain that their part of the wall would be strong. But of course, whenever people make a commitment to do the work of God there's going to be opposition and so it was as this building project got underway. The people who took over the land when the Jews were deported to Babylon, felt they had squatters-rights to the land and didn't want the Jews to spoil what they had been enjoying. So, these "squatters" did everything possible to stop the work. But Nehemiah pursued his plan of action and the walls were completed in record time – fifty-two days (Nehemiah 6:15).

Once the wall was completed, Nehemiah wanted to make certain that the people were going to focus on God, so he asked Ezra to read from the Law of Moses. When Ezra opened the book of the Law, the people stood and he began to read. Then the Levites instructed the people in the Law while the people were standing there. *"They read from the Book of the Law of God, making it clear and giving the meaning so that the people could understand what was being read"* (Nehemiah 8:8). Convicted of their sins when they heard God's Word being read, the people humbled themselves before God and confessed their sins, signing an agreement to obey the Law of Moses. Once we get to Nehemiah 13, the history of the Jewish nation is complete until the opening chapter of the Gospels.

In fact, here's something for you to do. Pick up a Bible and put one finger at Nehemiah 13 and another finger at Matthew 1. Hold tightly to your Bible and turn it upside down. Everything that is dangling between your two fingers belongs before Nehemiah 13 chronologically. In other words, if you were to put the books in chronological order, the dangling books would have to be placed somewhere before Nehemiah 13. By now you should recognize that our Bible was not put together in a chronological fashion.

However, there are other books written after the Exile that continue God's love story to mankind, including Haggai, Zechariah and Malachi, so let's consider each one of them.

HAGGAI (520 B.C.) – The Jews had returned to Jerusalem and they began to build the Temple under the leadership of their governor, Zerubbabel. However, due to the opposition from the *"land residents"* while the Jews were in Babylon, opposition arose and stopped the building program. The Jews then decided to invest their time in their own personal building projects. So, Haggai had to deal with people who had lost their zeal for the Lord and had turned to zeal for themselves.

This aroused the anger of the Lord, who wanted them to return to God's building program, so God raised up Haggai, who wrote, *"Give careful thought to your ways, go up into the mountains and bring down timber and build the house, so that I may take pleasure in it and be honored,' says the Lord. "You expected much, but see, it turned out to be little. What you brought home, I blew away. Why?' declares the Lord Almighty. 'Because of my house, which remains a ruin, while each of you is busy with his own house"'* (Haggai 1:7-9). So, God raised up Haggai to get the Jews to finish what they began when they started building the Temple.

Haggai uses a phrase four times in his Book to motivate his people to do what they first committed themselves to accomplish – *"Give careful thought to your ways"* (1:5,7, 15,18). It's a statement that should cause us to examine our own priorities. It is very easy look after our own needs and wants, as well as those of our family, but in the process, neglect the things that would bring us closer to the Lord, such as spending time with Him in prayer and the study of His Word. The Lord could certainly be telling each of us, including this author, *"Give careful thought to your ways"*. Is it possible that we are working harder and yet have nothing to show for it at the end of the day? Are we making more money this year than last, and yet it seems like there are always more weeks in the month than there is money to pay the bills?

How did Haggai continue God's story of love to His people? He encouraged them by saying, *"Be strong, all you people of the land, 'declares the Lord, and work. For I am with you,' declares the Lord Almighty."* (Haggai 2:4) And later, Haggai adds these words from the Lord to His people, *"From this day on I will bless you"* (Haggai 2:19). These words were the motivation that encouraged the people to complete the Temple, so they could worship the Lord who delivered them from Babylonian captivity and brought them back to the city to rebuild the Temple.

ZECHARIAH (520-518 B.C.) – While the Book of Haggai is only composed of two chapters, Zechariah has a lot more to say in fourteen chapters. Zechariah launched his ministry about two months after Haggai, so the people were hearing God's voice of love from more than one prophet. He was also both a prophet and a priest, coming from a priestly family.

As the first half of the Book deals with eight night visions, this last half emphasizes four messages (7:1-8:23) and two burdens (9:1-14:21), focusing on the Coming of Messiah.

And in the last chapter of Zechariah, the prophet goes into detail as to where Messiah, God's love in the flesh, will land when He does come and then describes some major geological changes that will occur. *"On that day his feet will stand on the Mount of Olives, east of Jerusalem, and the Mount of Olives will be split in two from east to west, forming a great valley, with half of the mountain moving north and half mobbing south. . . Jerusalem will be raised up and remain in its place"* (Zechariah 14:4,10). Now since this prophecy has never yet been fulfilled, I see it as an event which still lies in our future. As the Old Testament closes, God raises up one more prophet who prepares the way for the center focus of

His Love Story to mankind. That focus is His Son, Jesus Christ. Malachi predicts a forerunner to announce Messiah's arrival.

MALACHI – (430 B.C.) - While we do have sufficient information on most prophets, that is not the case when it comes to Malachi. But we do know that as he opens his message to those who have returned from captivity, he begins with these words from God – *"I have loved you' says the Lord'"* (Malachi 1:2). The people were questioning God's love, for they responded with, *"How have you loved us?"* Malachi continues his oracle explaining how God had demonstrated His love to His people time and again and then closes his prophecy with these words about one who would prepare Messiah's coming to earth, *"See, I will send my messenger, who will prepare the way before me. Then suddenly the Lord you are seeking will come to his temple; the messenger of the covenant whom you desire, will come,' says the Lord Almighty"* (Malachi 3:1-2).

It is the last Book of our Old Testament. When Malachi completed his prophecy, heaven's voice went dead. Four hundred years passed and there was silence from heaven. The prophets stopped speaking and the apostles had not yet been born.

The next voice man hears from heaven is that of an angel. He appeared to a priest in the temple and said, *"Do not be afraid, Zechariah; your prayer has been heard. Your wife Elizabeth will bear you a son, and you are to give him the name John. He will be a joy and delight to you, and many will rejoice because of his birth, for he will be great in the sight of the Lord . . . And he will go before the Lord, in the spirit and power of Elijah, to turn the hearts of the fathers to their children and the disobedient to the wisdom of the righteous – to make ready a people prepared for the Lord"* (Luke 1:13-14, 16-17).

Why is this important? Because it picks up where Malachi left off. That prophet's last words in print were, *"See,*

I will send my messenger, who will prepare the way before me. . .'See, I will send you the prophet Elijah before that great and dreadful day of the Lord comes. He will turn the hearts of the fathers to their children, and the hearts of the children to their fathers; or else I will come and strike the land with a curse''' (Malachi 3:1; 4:5).

The prophets' words over the past several hundred years were about to unfold before the eyes of those who were looking for a Messiah, as well as those who had no idea what a Messiah was. The last Book of the Old Testament introduces us to God's Plan, as it unfolds in the New Testament.

If we were to look at Israel's history from the Exile to the Return in chart form, it would look something like the following:

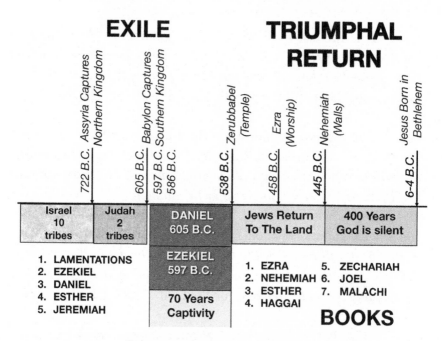

Figure 9 - Chart by Dr. Rick Yohn

Remember that what we've covered so far is only the first part of the Bible, though it is the larger of the two sections. We've had the opportunity to explore the Beginnings, Settlement, Kingdom, Exile and Triumphal Return of the Jews to the Land after a seventy-year captivity. Also, remember that we are talking about **HIS LOVE STORY**. God progressively revealed Himself and His love to man over the centuries, a little at a time. Now it's time to continue God's Love Story as it is revealed in the New Testament.

A LOVE STORY FROM GOD THROUGHOUT THE NEW TESTAMENT

7

God's Love Story in the Flesh

Contrast Between Old & New Testaments

OLD TESTAMENT	NEW TESTAMENT
• COVERS A PERIOD OF SEVERAL THOUSAND YEARS	• COVERS A PERIOD OF LESS THAN 100 YEARS
• PREDICTS THE COMING OF MESSIAH	• REVEALS THE MESSIAH'S ARRIVAL
• FOCUSES ON A NATION (ISRAEL)	• FOCUSES ON A PEOPLE (THE CHURCH)
• SINS COVERED BY THE BLOOD OF ANIMALS	• SINS REMOVED BY THE BLOOD OF JESUS CHRIST

Figure 10- Chart by Dr. Rick Yohn

New Testament Overview
THE GOSPELS
1. Matthew
2. Mark
3. Luke
4. John

HISTORY
1. Acts of the Apostles

EPISTLES (LETTERS)

1. Romans	12. Titus
2. 1Corinthians	13. Philemon
3. 2Corinthians	14. Hebrews
4. Galatians	15. James
5. Ephesians	16. 1Peter
6. Philippians	17. 2Peter
7. Colossians	18. 1John
8. 1Thessalonians	19. 2John
9. 2Thessalonians	20. 3John
10. 1Timothy	21. Jude
11. 2Timothy	

PROPHECY

1. Revelation

While the Old Testament begins God's Love story through creation, individuals, and the nation of Israel, the New Testament fully displays God's love to mankind in the person of His Son, Jesus Christ. He is the epitome of love. The Son of God is now introduced by the Gospel writers.

The Spirit of God directed four men to reveal the Person and Work of this Messiah (Anointed One), who was promised throughout the Old Testament. Each man had a different writing style, purpose and audience for his Gospel. But what is a Gospel? The word comes from the Greek word, **euaggelion**, which means *"good news"*. The Gospels present the good news that the Messiah has arrived and His name is Jesus.

Most people would consider these Gospel writers to be men of great character and trustworthy, and they would be right. But that was not the case in their early lives. If we were to choose four men to help someone understand who this Son of God was, what kind of men would we choose? Men who possess unquestionable religious credentials? Men who are highly educated? Men known for their writing skills over the years and are quite popular with the reading public of the first century? What about a hated tax collector, an unfaithful companion, or perhaps a fisherman? No? Well let's compare our criteria with the four men God chose to make His Son known to the world down through the centuries.

MATTHEW - Matthew wrote his Gospel primarily to the Jews. Godly Jews were looking for the promised Messiah to arrive. After all, did not the prophets of old predict where He would be born, where He would minister, and how He would be treated? Though various men appeared on the scene claiming to be the Messiah, they were proven to be false time and again. When Matthew took out his pen and began to write to the Jews about Jesus, he wanted them to see that Jesus indeed fulfilled many of the prophecies predicted by the prophets of the Old Testament, including the fact that Jesus was the King of the Jews.

But who was this Matthew? He was a former tax collector and hated by many of the Jews, because he worked for the Romans. Most of the tax collectors were considered unscrupulous thieves. They would charge the Jews more than the Romans required. Then they would pay the Romans what was due and keep the overcharge for themselves. Before he met the Messiah, Matthew went by the name of Levi. That was an honorable name if you were a Jew because the priests came from the tribe of Levi. But just by his occupation, this Levi seemed to be defaming that honorable name.

One day Levi was collecting taxes in a town called Capernaum. Rumor had it that a man living in this town claimed to be the promised Messiah. He also heard stories about the miracles and the teachings of this man. And then the day arrived when this special teacher confronted Levi by walking up to Levi's tax booth and challenging this hated man to follow Him. So, impressed by what he saw and heard by this man, Levi left his occupation of tax-collecting and followed Jesus from that day forward.

MARK - **Mark's** story is quite different. A godly mother who held a home church in her house reared Mark in the fear (reverence) of the Lord. He even went on a mission tour with the Apostle Paul and his cousin, Barnabas. However, in the early days of the trip, he got homesick and left Paul and Barnabas, returning home. Many months later, when Paul was preparing to go on another mission journey, Barnabas suggested that they give Mark a second chance and take him with them. Paul was furious at the suggestion, resulting in a rift between these two godly men.

So, Paul chose another man for the trip named Silas, while Barnabas took his cousin with him back to his home, somewhere on the Isle of Cyprus. But Barnabas was not Mark's only mentor. Another man affected the life of Mark. He was known as the Apostle Peter. As Mark matured and spent a lot of time with Peter, the Apostle shared much of the teachings and character of Jesus that he personally experienced during those three years with the Savior. Eventually Mark used much of the information that he gleaned from Peter and wrote the Gospel of Mark, presenting Jesus as a servant. Mark's Gospel was also written primarily for the Greeks. And remember the Apostle Paul's first reaction to Mark when he refused to give him a second chance? Listen to what Paul says near the end of his life as he sits in a dungeon, awaiting execution. He writes to young Timothy and asks him a favor – *"Only Luke is with me. Get Mark and bring him with you, because he is helpful to me in my ministry"* (2Timothy 4:11). Mark, the runaway? Mark, that scoundrel that left you in the lurch on that first missionary journey? *"Yes, he is helpful to me in my ministry"*

God's Love Story in the Flesh

LUKE - The Third Gospel writer was unlike Matthew, Mark and John. His name was **Luke.** He was a companion with the Apostle Paul, traveling with him on many of Paul's missionary journeys. He was also highly educated. When he wrote his Gospel, Luke used a higher level of the Greek language, almost classical. He was also known to be a doctor and a historian.

Throughout his Gospel, Luke describes Jesus as the Son of Man. This was a term used by the prophet Daniel (Daniel 7) and it focuses on Jesus' humanity. His audience was more of a Gentile ethnicity and he is probably the only Gentile writer of any book of the Bible. All the other writers were Jews. Luke also wrote the Book of Acts.

JOHN - Then there was **John**. What can we say about this man? Early in life, John and his brother James were known as *"the sons of thunder"*. They possessed a volatile temper. It didn't take much to set them off. On one occasion, as the two were walking with Jesus through a town in Samaria, a group of Samaritans were yelling at them. Both brothers asked the Lord permission to call fire down from heaven and devour the people.

This story reminds me of the times I've walked Buddy, my Golden Retriever. He is gentle and loving, with an insatiable desire to be accepted by all with whom he comes into contact. However, when someone walks toward us with a small dog on the leash, the little creature strains at the leash and launches ear-piercing challenges to big, lovable Buddy. The little dog's master usually yells at the dog and yanks the dog back into position.

That's the scene I capture in this account of James and John. Like the little dog, they see something they don't like and immediately want to destroy the problem on sight. So, Jesus captures their attention and refocuses it on His purpose and plan.

Therefore, Luke tells us, *"But Jesus turned and rebuked them, and they went to another village"* (Luke 9:55).

That was then, but Jesus made such an impact on the two brothers, that John became known as *"the one whom Jesus loved"*. That's not to say that Jesus had no love for the other disciples, but rather, John was the one whom Jesus entrusted with His mother. As our Lord was dying on the cross, John was the only disciple who did not run away from the authorities. Instead, John took Mary, the mother of Jesus, to the foot of the cross to see her son. As the two of them looked up at the bloodied body of our Lord, Jesus saw the two figures below Him. As He continued to gaze at them, Jesus' eyes widened as He recognized that He was looking down at both His mother and the one apostle who refused to run away. The Lord first spoke to His mother and said, *"Dear woman, here is your son"*. Then He looked at John and said, *"Here is your mother"*. (John 26-27).

Widows of that day often ended up impoverished, for they had no one to care for them. Our Lord's last act was to entrust his mother into the hands of the one disciple who was willing to bring her to the foot of the cross. Some wonder why Jesus didn't use the term *"mother"*, which to us sounds more endearing. But the word that Jesus used was an endearing term. Tradition tells us that John took Mary with him to the city of Ephesus (in present-day Turkey). He later became the pastor of that great church and is buried there. His Gospel is unique in many ways. You will see in the following chart that, 92% of his material is unique to his Gospel when compared with the other three. John is writing to all mankind and immediately identifies this man as God in the flesh.

All four Gospels inform the reader that Jesus is the fulfillment of many prophecies found in the Old Testament, including where this Messiah would be born, where He would minister, the special powers that He would demonstrate, His teaching style (parables), His death and resurrection and many other events in the life of the Lord.

THE FOUR GOSPELS
(EZEKIEL 1:10; REVELATION 4:7)

	MATTHEW	MARK	LUKE	JOHN
PORTRAIT	*LION* KING	*OX* SERVANT	*MAN* SON OF MAN	*EAGLE* GOD
AUDIENCE	JEWS	ROMANS	GREEKS	MANKIND
KEYWORDS	Fulfill(ed) 15 times	Immediately 11 times	Son of Man 25 times	Believe 54 times
EMPHASIS	SERMONS	MIRACLES	PARABLES	ALLEGORIES
UNIQUE CONTENT	42%	7%	59%	92%
O.T. QUOTES	53	36	25	20

"Talk Through The Bible" – Bruce Wilkinson & Kenneth Boa, Thomas Nelson Publishers, 1983

Now let's turn to the Life of Christ. Where do you begin when talking about our Lord? The Apostle John even threw up his hands after writing his great Gospel and wrote, *"Jesus did many other things as well. If every one of them were written down, I suppose that even the whole world would not have room for the books that would be written"* (John 21:25).

Let's now focus on a chronological perspective of the life and ministry of our Lord Jesus Christ, beginning with some of the announcements concerning His arrival to earth.

Prophetic Announcements

THE PROPHET - The righteous Jews were looking for Messiah's arrival for centuries. Some were holding the words of Moses in their hearts when he told his people, *"The Lord your God will raise up for you a prophet like me from among your own brothers. You must listen to him"* (Deuteronomy 18:15). When Jesus did arrive and minister, the people began to ask questions and draw conclusions. *"After the people saw the miraculous sign that Jesus did, they began to say, 'Surely this is the Prophet who is to come into the world'"* (John 6:14)

BORN OF A VIRGIN – The Prophet Isaiah predicted, *"Therefore the Lord himself will give you a sign: The virgin will be with child and will give birth to a son and will call him Immanuel"* (Isaiah 7:14). How many virgins have ever given birth to a child? When Joseph, Mary's future husband discovered that she was pregnant, he decided to quietly divorce her. But an angel interceded and appeared to Joseph and said, *"Joseph son of David, do not be afraid to take Mary home as your wife, because what is conceived in her is from the Holy Spirit. She will give birth to a son, and you are to give him the name Jesus, because he will save his people from their sins"* (Matthew 1:20-21).

BORN IN BETHLEHEM – The Prophet Micah predicted hundreds of years before Jesus arrived that Messiah would be born in Bethlehem. He wrote, *"But you, Bethlehem Ephrathah, though you are small among the clans of Judah, out of you will come for me one who will be ruler over Israel, whose origins are from of old, from ancient times"* (Micah 5:2). That was the prediction, so in what town was Jesus born? Matthew answers this question when he writes, *"After Jesus was born in Bethlehem in Judea, during the time of King Herod, Magi from the east came to Jerusalem and asked,*

'Where is the one who has been born king of the Jews? We saw his star in the east and have come to worship him'" (Matthew 2:1-2).

MINISTRY AROUND THE SEA OF GALILEE – The Prophet Isaiah predicted that a great light would shine in the area where this Messiah would come. Listen to Isaiah's description of that area. We might think that he was looking at someone's GPS – *"Nevertheless, there will be no more gloom for those who were in distress. In the past he humbled the land of Zebulun and the land of Naphtali, but in the future he will honor Galilee of the Gentiles by the way of the sea, along the Jordan – The people walking in darkness have seen a great light, on those living in the land of the shadow of death a light has dawned"* (Isaiah 9:1-2).

Galilee of the Gentiles - Now without a map, the above two verses are a bunch of gobbledygook! What in the world was Isaiah talking about? Let's look at some history. As we took our journey through the Old Testament we stated that the Assyrians came down to Israel, the Northern Kingdom, and removed the people from the Land and repopulated the Land with Gentiles. Therefore, what was once Jewish Galilee now became known as *"Galilee of the Gentiles"*. Spiritual darkness covered the area with pagan worship. The remnant of Israel was living in deep spiritual darkness without the Scriptures.

Zebulun and Naphtali - We also learn that the tribe of Zebulun and the tribe of Naphtali possessed land in that same area. The key town in Zebulun was the town of Nazareth, where Jesus lived and the key town in Naphtali was the town of Capernaum, where Jesus ministered and lived for three years.

The Sea and the Jordan River – To what Sea was Isaiah referring? There is only one body of fresh water in that area and it is the Sea of Galilee.

Figure 11 - By 12 tribus de Israel.svg: Translated by Kordas12 staemme
israels heb.svg: by user: 12 staemme israels.png: by user:Janzderivative
work: Richardprins (talk) - 12 tribus de Israel.svg12 staemme israels
heb.svg12 staemme israels.png, CC BY-SA 3.0, https://commons
.wikimedia.org/w/index.php?curid=10865624

Have seen a Great Light – Who walked around that Lake for three years? The One who called Himself *"the light of the world"* (John 8:12). Before Jesus arrived in Capernaum, the Jews in the area walked in spiritual darkness. But when the Light of the world arrived and preached about repentance and the Kingdom of God, spiritual darkness began to dissipate.

To link everything together, look at the Gospel of Matthew where the writer penned, *"Leaving Nazareth he went and lived in Capernaum, which was by the lake in the area of Zebulun and Naphtali – to fulfill what was said through the prophet Isaiah: 'Land of Zebulun and land of Naphtali, the way to the sea, along the Jordan, Galilee of the Gentiles - the people living in darkness have seen a great light on those living in the land of the shadow of death a light has dawned'"* (Matthew 4:13-15).

Most of Jesus' ministry was around the Sea of Galilee, the only body of fresh water in Israel. It is not a Sea, but rather a lake and has four different names: (1) the Sea of Galilee (the region around the Lake); (2) the Lake of Gennasaret (the Plain on the West side of the Lake and the Greek word for harp); (3) the Lake of Kinneret (Hebrew name for *"harp"*, since the lake looks like a harp); and (4) the Sea of Tiberias (the largest city on the Sea of Galilee). The town in which Jesus spent most of His time was Capernaum, the home of Peter.

There are so many other prophecies concerning Jesus arrival and ministry on earth, but let's look at His early, middle and late ministry.

The Early Ministry Of Jesus Christ

For the first thirty years of His life, Jesus was unnoticed. Nobody knew His name. He could move in and out of synagogues, in and out of the Temple, walk past Jewish leaders and no one noticed His presence. He was respected in His hometown of Nazareth and was not considered to be anything other than a young man who cared for His mother, since Joseph was most likely deceased by the time Jesus began to minister.

BAPTISM - Then came His baptism that took place in the southern part of Israel, across from Jericho and on the other side of the Jordan River (present day Country of Jordan). Down there the Jordan River is not the clear water that you find up in the north where many tourists today get baptized. By the time the Jordan reaches Bethany across the Jordan, it is muddy, having washed everything from the north down to the south. John the Baptist, Jesus' cousin, baptized the Lord.

TEMPTATION - Immediately after His baptism, the Spirit of the Lord drove Him out into the desert, where He was tempted forty days and forty nights by the devil himself. Each time the devil came to Him, Jesus quoted from the Scriptures and said, *"It is written"*. The Lord defeated the devil on his own turf, earth. He used the same weapons that we have, to defeat the devil: (1) The Scriptures; (2) Prayer and (3) The power of the Holy Spirit. All three weapons are available to each one of us. The more we know God's Word and apply its principles to our lives, the better we'll be able to deal with the daily temptations that we face.

Secondly, the more time we spend with the Lord in prayer, the more effective we will be when those temptations confront us, especially when we are least expecting them. And thirdly, we have as much of the Holy Spirit as Jesus had. He doesn't come to us in percentages or installments. When we receive Jesus Christ as our Savior, we simultaneously receive the Holy Spirit who comes to live within us. He is there to empower us to live a life pleasing to God. He can empower us to say *"No"* to temptation. In fact, the writer to the Hebrews writes this about Jesus – *"For we do not have a high priest who is unable to sympathize with our weaknesses, but we have one who has been tempted in every way, just as we are – yet was without sin"* (Hebrews 4:15).

When we are tempted, we may feel that there is no way out. We may think that the temptation is so powerful, we must give in to it. But I have good news. Every temptation has its own escape hatch. How do I know that? Because the Bible makes it very clear that we face the same kinds of temptations, though it may not be the exact temptation. Some things that are more tempting to me may not be that tempting to you. And whatever the temptation might be, we can get out of it. The Apostle Paul reminds us, *"No temptation has seized you except what is common to man. And God is faithful; he will not let you be tempted beyond what you can bear. But when you are tempted, **he will also provide a way out** so that you can stand up under it"* (1 Corinthians 10:13). That's quite a promise. No matter what the temptation, God always provides a way out.

Once the Lord was baptized and then defeated the temptations of the devil in the wilderness, He began to call His disciples, beginning with some who were disciples of John the Baptist.

Jesus' Galilee Ministry

Calling His Disciples – *"The next day John saw Jesus coming toward him and said, 'Look, the Lamb of God who takes away the sin of the world'"* (John 1:20). The following day John saw Jesus once again and cried out, *"Look, the Lamb of God"* (John1:36). These two statements captured the attention of Andrew, one of John's disciples and he began to follow Jesus. *"Turning around, Jesus saw them following and asked, 'what do you want?' They said, 'Rabbi' (which means Teacher), where are you staying?' 'Come,' he replied, 'and you will see'"* (John 1:38-39).

From this meeting, Jesus met and called both Peter and Nathaniel. Later Jesus saw a tax collector by the name of Levi, sitting at a tax booth in the city of Capernaum. The Lord went over to him and said, *"Follow me"*. Levi got up and never looked back. We know him better by the name of Matthew, the Gospel writer. Eventually Jesus called twelve men to live, eat and travel with him. That group included fishermen, political zealots, a tax collector and two brothers, each with a short temper. He also chose one who would betray Him by turning Him over to the authorities. He was a thief in sheep's clothing. His name was Judas.

Jesus' Later Ministry

Jesus' later ministry begins to unfold in Matthew 11 where Jesus began to denounce the three cities around the northern part of the Sea of Galilee. These were the cities that saw the "great light that had dawned", Jesus Christ. However, they rejected His message and so the Lord brought a curse on all three towns – *"Woe to you, **Korazin**! Woe to you, **Bethsaida**! If the miracles that were performed in you had been performed in Tyre and Sidon, they would have repented long ago in sackcloth and ashes. But I tell you, it will be more bearable for Tyre and Sidon on the day of judgment than for you. And you, **Capernaum**, will you be lifted up to the skies? No, you will go down to the depths"* (Matthew 11:21-23).

Then in chapter 12, the Pharisees accuse Jesus of casting out demons by the power of Beelzebub. By the time you get to Matthew 13, the Lord begins to speak in parables, hiding understanding from those who have rejected Him and revealing truth to those who believed in Him.

Then the Lord leads the disciples on a journey into Gentile territory. After feeding the 5,000 Jews on the west side of the Sea of Galilee, the Lord and His disciples go to the east side of the Sea into Gentile territory, where Jesus feeds 4,000 Gentiles. He then takes them up to Caesarea Philippi and asks them that all important question, *"Who do men say that I am?"* Peter alone gives the correct answer – *"You are the Christ, the Son of the living God"* (Matthew 16:16).

Following this experience, the Lord and His disciples hike up a high mountain, most likely Mount Hermon, and is *"transfigured"* before their eyes. They not only see Jesus, but also Moses and Elijah. Peter becomes so excited about what he sees that he wants to build booths for the three of them. And after this experience, Jesus begins to focus on His final ministry. The Gospel of Luke tells us, *"As the time approached for him to be taken up to heaven, Jesus resolutely set out for Jerusalem"* (Luke 9:51). Jesus now withdraws from Galilee, though He does make a few brief trips back to the area.

If we follow Luke's account, we'll see Jesus heading for Jerusalem. He first enters a Samaritan village on His way to Jerusalem (Luke 9:51-53). Next, we find the Lord going through villages and towns, teaching *"as he made his way to Jerusalem"* (Luke 13:22). We pick up the story in chapter 17, where we read, *"Now on his way to Jerusalem, Jesus traveled along the border between Samaria and Galilee"* (Luke 17:11). And in chapter 19 we are told, *"While they were listening to this, he went on to tell them a parable, because he was near Jerusalem and the people thought that the kingdom of God was going to appear at once"* (Luke 19:11). And finally, in this same chapter, Jesus rides into Jerusalem on a donkey (Luke 19:28-44).

At this point, the Lord spends His last week in the City where God chose to place His Name and where God dwelt in a very special way, above the Ark of the Covenant between the Cherubim, within the Holy of Holies in the Temple. The Lord taught in the Temple courts, and after His time in the upper room with His disciples, where He gave a very informative message (John 13-17), He and His disciples crossed the Kidron Valley to the Mount of Olives.

Olives. That evening, Jesus was taken, brought before the high priest and experienced a mock trial and then sent to Pontius Pilate for the death penalty to be carried out.

Our Lord was beaten and crucified. The Jewish leaders said that was because of His blasphemy against God. But the Scriptures allow us to see that Jesus' crucifixion was part of a Divine Plan between the Father and the Son. Jesus was God's sin bearer who took our sin upon Himself, so we might enjoy life forever with God.

After the Lord's death and burial, He rose from the dead three days later and appeared to many over a fifty-day period. In fact, on one occasion, over 500 men saw the Lord personally (1 Corinthians 15:6). But that's not the end of the story. The Lord had made a promise to His disciples in the Upper Room – *"In my Father's house are many rooms; if it were not so, I would have told you. I am going there to prepare a place for you. And if I go and prepare a place for you, I will come back and take you to be with me that you also may be where I am"* (John 14:2-3).

And as the Gospels close, the Book of Acts opens. And in the first chapter of that Book, Jesus ascends into heaven while the disciples gaze at His exit from earth and His ascent into the heavens. And as they watch the Lord disappear, two men suddenly appear, dressed in white. They tell the disciples, *"Men of Galilee, they said, 'why do you stand here looking into the sky? This same Jesus, who has been taken from you into heaven will come back in the same way you have seen him go into heaven'"* (Acts 1:11).

Remember where they were standing at the time? The Mount of Olives (Acts 1:12). And not only will Jesus return in the same way that He left (bodily), but also to the same place where He left, the Mount of Olives. How do we know this? Listen to the prophet Zechariah whom we quoted previously, *"On that day his feet will stand on the Mount of Olives, east of Jerusalem, and the Mount of Olives will be split in two from east to west, forming a great valley, with half of the mountain moving north and half moving south"* (Zechariah 14:4).

While the **Gospels** focus on the birth, ministry, death and resurrection of our Lord, the **Book of Acts** reveals the founding, development and expansion of the Church. The **Epistles**, letters to churches and individuals, explain and expand on the Gospels about the identity of Jesus, as well as encourage two young pastors (Timothy and Titus) and deal with issues in the early Church. And the Book of **Revelation**, sometimes referred to as the Apocalypse, is a prophetic Book and deals primarily with future events.

8

The Story Expanded (Acts)

After we leave the Gospels that tell us about this man Jesus, we come to the Book of Acts. This Book is an historical record of what occurred after Jesus ascended into heaven. The writer of this Book is the same man who wrote the Gospel of Luke. In fact, it is believed that at one time the Gospel of Luke and the Book of Acts were one book. Why? Not only because you have the same author, but also because Acts picks up where the Gospel of Luke ended. Furthermore, it was written, not only by the same author, but also to the same individual. Look at the first few verses of each Book.

*"Many have undertaken to draw up an account of the things that have been fulfilled among us, ² just as they were handed down to us by those who from the first were eyewitnesses and servants of the word. ³ Therefore, since I myself have carefully investigated everything from the beginning, it seemed good also to me to write an orderly account for you, **most excellent Theophilus**, ⁴ so that you may know the certainty of the things you have been taught."* (Luke 1:1-4)

*"In my **former book**, **Theophilus**, I wrote about all that Jesus began to do and to teach ² until the day he was taken up to heaven, after giving instructions through the Holy Spirit to the apostles he had chosen. ³ After his suffering, he showed himself to these men and gave many convincing proofs that he was alive. He appeared to them over a period of forty days and spoke about the kingdom of God."* (Acts 1:1-3)

We see that Luke wanted to continue the Jesus Story after His resurrection. The question that Theophilus may have been asking might be, *"Now that Jesus was crucified, buried and resurrected, is that it? Is that the end of the story or is there more?"* Yes, there is a lot more to the story. Let me tell you what happened soon after Jesus' resurrection. Luke proceeds to tell Theophilus the rest of the story.

"On one occasion, while he was eating with them, he gave them this command: 'Do not leave Jerusalem, but wait for the gift my Father promised, which you have heard me speak about. ⁵ For John baptized with water, but in a few days you will be baptized with the Holy Spirit.' ⁶ So when they met together, they asked him, 'Lord, are you at this time going to restore the kingdom to Israel?' ⁷ He said to them: 'It is not for you to know the times or dates the Father has set by his own authority. ⁸ But you will receive power when the Holy Spirit comes on you; and you will be my witnesses in Jerusalem, and in all Judea and Samaria, and to the ends of the earth'" (Acts 1:4-8).

However, over the years, the Church considered Luke as part of the Gospels and the history of Jesus. They also viewed the Book of Acts as the history of the Church. And though Acts is the history of the founding and growth of the Church, it is also a continuation of the account of Jesus, God's ultimate expression of love, who commissioned His disciples to take what they had seen and heard to the nations.

Why is it called Acts? Because it tells the reader about the spread of the Gospel and it includes some of the Apostles, such as John, Peter and Paul. And though many see it as the Acts of the Apostles, behind the scenes, you could more accurately call this Book the Acts of the Holy Spirit through the Apostles.

At this point, Luke provides us with an outline for the entire Book of Acts. He tells Theophilus that Jesus commissioned the disciples (apostles) to take His message to the ends of the earth, beginning right there in Jerusalem. When we read through this Book, we will see that it is divided into three major sections:

I. THE GOSPEL IS PREACHED IN **JERUSALEM**
(Acts 1:9-8:3)
II. THE GOSPEL IS PREACHED IN **JUDEA AND SAMARIA**
(Acts 8:4-11:18)
III. THE GOSPEL IS PREACHED THROUGHOUT **THE KNOWN WORLD**
(ACTS 11:19-28:31)

Jerusalem was still reeling from the past two months. The Jewish leaders were attempting to get their house back in order and the people settled and focused on them as the authorities for both religious and civil order. But soon after Jesus ascended into heaven, Peter, the disciple who denied that he ever knew the Lord, was back on the street warning the people to repent of their sin and recognize Jesus as their Savior (Acts 2:14-40).

They Took The Gospel To Jerusalem (Acts 1:9-8:3)

There are three key individuals in this section. First there is the risen Lord Jesus Christ. Over a 50-day period He meets with His disciples, demonstrating time and again that death has no control over Him. He has conquered death (Acts 1:1-11).

The second key individual is the Apostle Peter. Though he had recently denied the Lord, Peter rose to the occasion. He stood before the masses and proclaimed the resurrected Christ. And then from Jerusalem, Peter obeyed the Lord and went up to Caesarea to a Gentile clientele, including a Roman soldier in charge of 100 men. There he preached to a group of people within the Centurion's household and they came to faith in Christ (Acts 1:12-12:25).

Finally, the third key figure to appear on the scene is a man named Saul. He was a persecutor of the Church, but He met the Master on his way to Damascus. It was on that road where he found that the one he had been persecuting was Jesus Christ. So, Saul's name is changed to Paul and he becomes a great defender of the faith (Acts 13-28).

What we read about in the Book of Acts is the continuation of a promise made to a man 2,000 years earlier. God promised this man Abraham that he would not only be the father of many nations, but that all the nations of the world would be blessed through him (Genesis 12:1-3). The beginning of the blessing emerges in the birth of Christ (the Gospel of Luke) and continues through the emerging body of believers known as the Church (the Book of Acts), made up of not only Jews, but also Gentiles.

The Apostle Paul reveals this "mystery" of Jew and Gentile in one body of believers as he pens these words to the Church at Ephesus – *"In reading this, then, you will be able to understand my insight into the mystery of Christ, which was not made known to men in other generations as it has now been revealed by the Spirit to God's holy apostles and prophets. This mystery is that through the gospel the Gentiles are heirs together with Israel, members together of one body, and sharers together in the promise in Christ Jesus"* (Ephesians 3:4-6). That's what the Book of Acts is all about – fulfilling the promise to Abraham when He made a Covenant with him, known as the Abrahamic Covenant.

They Took The Gospel To Judea And Samaria (Acts 8:4-11:18)

In a short time, 5,000 believers were added to this new organism, known first as people of the Way and then its members were called "Christians" in a city known as Antioch in Syria. Just when the religious leaders thought they had solved their problem of this man who claimed to be the Messiah, the Son of the living God, conversions to the Way were occurring every day. So, the leaders decide to squelch this threat to their authority and position. They began to persecute the fledgling church. We read in this Book, *"On that day a great persecution broke out against the church at Jerusalem, and all except the apostles were scattered throughout Judea and Samaria"* (Acts 8:1). Why would God allow one of the new deacons by the name of Stephen to preach a great sermon, be stoned to death (Acts 6-7) and then permit a great persecution of believers in Jerusalem?

We can answer that question from a principle in the Old Testament. Recall the story of Joseph, who had been sold as a slave by his brothers and taken to Egypt, where he was falsely accused of an act he did not commit and thrown in jail for years. Why would God allow such a bad thing to happen to such a good man? Let's let Joseph give us the reason in his own words. After he had become the second in command in Egypt and brought his entire family to live in Egypt, including those scoundrel siblings of his, he told them, *"You intended to harm me, but God intended it for good to accomplish what is now being done, the saving of many lives"* (Genesis 50:20). If his brothers had not been jealous of him and sold him to a caravan on its way to Egypt, he never would have had the opportunity to be second in command in Egypt and save his family and many others from starvation, due to a great drought throughout the land.

What happened in the days of Joseph repeated itself in the days of the Apostles. The religious leaders were jealous of this growing church and the thousands of people turning away from them and trusting in Jesus Christ as their Savior and Lord. Therefore, they decided to persecute anyone who claimed to be a follower of Jesus. They put them in prison and killed many other believers. Hoping to extinguish the flame that was lit on the Day of Pentecost, they encouraged the explosion of the gospel to penetrate throughout the entire known world, even into the household of Caesar (Philippians 4:22).

They Took The Gospel Throughout The Known World (Acts 11:19-28:31)

Peter had already reached out to the Gentiles when he went to the home of Cornelius, the Roman Centurion living in Caesarea. Now it was Paul's turn to come on the scene. This great Apostle was introduced to the others by a man named Barnabas. I love the name because it means *"son of encouragement"*. Barnabas was the type of person who loved to connect people to one another. If anyone felt down and discouraged, this was the man who came alongside that individual and encouraged him.

Before Paul became known as the Apostle to the Gentiles, he was a zealot for the religious establishment. He was a Pharisee and was determined to snuff out this new threat to Judaism. But a funny thing happened on his way to Damascus, Syria. He had planned to persecute these new Christians by throwing them in jail, but in the process, he met the One whom he was persecuting, the risen Jesus Christ.

At that time, he was known as Saul of Tarsus. Let's listen to his story as he shares it with the believers in Galatia. He writes, *"But when God, who set me apart from birth and called me by his grace, was pleased to reveal his Son in me so that I might preach him among the Gentiles, I did not consult any man, nor did I go up to Jerusalem to see those who were apostles before I was, but I went immediately into Arabia and later returned to Damascus. Then after three years, I went up to Jerusalem to get acquainted with Peter and stayed with him fifteen days. I saw none of the other apostles - only James, the Lord's brother. I assure you before God that what I am writing you is not lie. Later I went to Syria and Cilicia. I was personally unknown to the churches of Judea that are in Christ"* (Galatians 1:15-22).

How did the Apostles accept this persecutor of the Church? The Book of Acts tells the story – *"When he came to Jerusalem, he tried to join the disciples, but they were all afraid of him, not believing that he really was a disciple. But Barnabas took him and brought him to the apostles"* (Acts 9:26-27). Everyone was afraid of Saul, but Barnabas put his own reputation on the line and brought him to the Apostles, who finally accepted him. Today we can thank Barnabas for our understanding of Christ. Why? Because without a Barnabas, there never would have been an Apostle Paul. That also means that thirteen of the twenty-seven books of the New Testament would never have been written.

Once the Apostle Paul is accepted by the rest of the Apostles, the Holy Spirit makes it known to the believers that He has set apart Barnabas and Saul for the next phase of the divine plan (Acts 13:2), which was to take the gospel to the Gentile world, which includes most of us today. The rest of the Book of Acts unfolds three major missionary journeys of Paul.

THE FIRST JOURNEY – Paul and Barnabas traveled through Cyprus and the eastern part of present day Turkey. He and Barnabas spoke in the synagogues, revealing that Jesus is truly the Messiah promised in the Old Testament Scriptures. They also preached to the Gentiles and many of them trusted in Christ as their Savior. Then they returned to Antioch in Syria and shared with the believers all that God was doing among both Jew and Gentile (Acts 14:21-28).

THE SECOND JOURNEY – Some time later Paul decided that it was time to once again take a journey back into what is now present day Turkey. Only this time it would be an extended journey. Barnabas thought that would be a great idea and added one other caveat – to take young John Mark with them. Remember that name? Let's revisit and expand on the story about this person called John Mark. However, Paul wanted nothing to do with this young man because he left them on the first journey and ran home.

Paul was focused on a mission, while Barnabas was focused on a person, his cousin John Mark. The dispute between the two men grew into a heated confrontation to the point where Barnabas decided to leave Paul and take Mark to Cyprus, the home of Barnabas. Therefore, Paul chose another man named Silas and the two of them made the next two journeys together. This time they travelled back to where Paul had been previously, but then continued their tour throughout present day Turkey, entering Asia Minor with the Gospel and even going so far as Macedonia and various

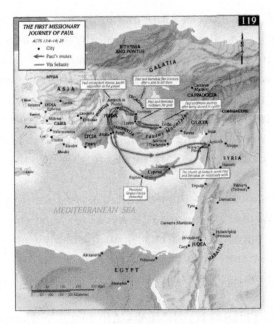

**Figure 12 - Briscoe, Thomas V. 1998. Nashville, TN: Holman
Bible Atlas, p. 244**

cities throughout Greece. They went to places like Thessalonica, Athens, Corinth, Ephesus and then to Jerusalem. In fact, Paul stayed in Corinth for a year and a half, teaching them the word of God. Later, Paul returned to Antioch of Syria. After some time, he was prepared to make a third journey.

But what about Barnabas and John Mark? Was God also able to bless them? Let's look at the events which unfolded, but not recorded in the Book of Acts. Barnabas spent several years mentoring and encouraging young John Mark. In fact, he did such a great job building into his life, that near the end of Paul's life as a prisoner in Rome, the Apostle wrote these words to another young man named Timothy, a pastor who had traveled with the Apostle on several occasions – *"Do your best to come to me quickly, for Demas because he loved this world, has deserted me and has gone to Thessalonica. Crescens has gone to Galatia, and Titus to Dalmatia.*

141

Only Luke is with me. Get Mark and bring him with you, because he is helpful to me in my ministry" (2Timothy 4:9-11). What a change of attitude in the Apostle Paul! Earlier Paul wanted nothing to do with John Mark and now he asks Timothy to be sure and send Mark to him because he viewed Mark as someone who was helpful to him in his ministry. What changed? Paul's perspective of Mark. John Mark went from the *"unwanted"* list to the *"wanted"* list for the Apostle Paul. In fact, Mark moved further into the *"needed"* list.

We should also thank Barnabas for John Mark. Not only did Barnabas give us the Apostle Paul, but he also gave us a very useful man named John Mark. You probably know this young man by his second name, Mark. Yes, the writer of the Gospel of Mark. Without Barnabas, we would have had three Gospels rather than four.

THE THIRD JOURNEY – After Paul had spent some time in Antioch, Syria, the Apostle once again set out on a third journey. This time he went to the region of Galatia and Phrygia and then on to Ephesus. At that point, Paul spent two years in Ephesus and reached so many for Christ that we are told, *". . . all the Jews and Greeks who lived in the province of Asia heard the word of the Lord"* (Acts 19:10).

However, because so many people were coming to faith in Jesus Christ, the silversmith trade was at risk. Concerned about the loss of revenue to the trade, a man named Demetrius, who made silver shrines of Artemis, called other tradesmen together, resulting in a riot at the theater in Ephesus. Paul was forced out of the city and headed up into Macedonia, where he stayed three months. From there he traveled to Troas, sailed on to Miletus and called for the Ephesian elders to whom he gave a farewell address and then sailed up to Tyre and then down to Caesarea on the coast of the Mediterranean. From there Paul went up to Jerusalem, where he was arrested. Later, he was taken back to Caesarea and eventually

**Figure 13 - Briscoe, Thomas V. 1998. Nashville, TN: Holman
Bible Atlas, p. 249**

taken as a prisoner to Rome. While in Rome, he spent the next two years under house arrest (Acts 28:16). After that time, Paul was sentenced to death.

What was this Apostle's attitude during these last two years of his life? The answer to that question can be found in one of his letters that he wrote while in prison. He told the believers at Philippi, *"For to me, to live is Christ and to die is gain. If I am to go on living in the body, this will mean fruitful labor for me. Yet what shall I choose? I do not know! I am torn between the two: I desire to depart and be with Christ, which is better by far; but it is more necessary for you that I remain in the body"* (Philippians 1:21-22).

One day we will all face the prospect of death. It's interesting that we all want to go to heaven, but we don't want to die to get there. Death is one topic that most of us never talk about. Too morbid? For some yes. Too scary? For most of us, yes. But there is a third attitude and perspective. That's the one this Apostle chose to adopt. He was aware that he would most likely be beheaded. Yes, he may feel the solid steel momentarily. However, he focused on the split second after his soul departed his body – standing in the presence of the One for Whom he had suffered. He was prepared to die for the God who loved him, despite his persecution of the church, despite his pride, despite his earlier hatred of Christians. That is what agape love is about – unconditional, unmerited love. Bowing before the throne of the One who loved him first, Paul finally heard the words," Well *done good and faithful servant*". This same man was now prepared to demonstrate his love by not shrinking back from reality, but rather by anticipating the joy that lay just on the other side of the blade.

Paul's time in house arrest at Rome closes out this wonderful continuation of the Jesus story that began with a promise to Abraham and was repeated time and again through the Old Testament Prophets. Then it was fulfilled throughout the Gospels and finally explained in the Epistles. And that is where we turn next, moving from five historical books to twenty-two letters to individuals and churches. I include the Book of Revelation for it is also a letter addressed to seven churches in Asia Minor and speaks about this exalted Savior as a lamb that was slain, the Lion of Judah, the King of Kings and Lord of Lords.

9

The Story Explained
(Paul's letters)

W e've just traveled through five historical Books of the New Testament that first announced Messiah's arrival, ministry, death and resurrection. We then moved on to the Book of Acts that continued and proclaimed *"the rest of the story"*. The message of the Gospel began in Jerusalem, moved north into Judea and Samaria and then west to the nations of the known world.

But now it is time to delve into the Epistles, letters written to explain to the world the identity of this man whom they called Jesus. The church was still young. False teachers had already invaded the churches and the young believers needed to hear from an authority figure whom they could trust to set the record straight. Was Jesus just a man who claimed to be God or was He God in the flesh? God chose six men to answer this and many other questions that arose in the minds and hearts of this new body of believers called the church. But let's first capture a glimpse of.

PAUL	UNKNOWN	JAMES	PETER	JUDE	JOHN
Romans	*Hebrews*	*James*	*1 Peter*	*Jude*	*1 John*
1 Corinthians			*2 Peter*		*2 John*
2 Corinthians					*3 John*
Galatians					
Ephesians					
Philippians					
Colossians					
1 Thessalonians					
2 Thessalonians					
1 Timothy					
2 Timothy					
Titus					
Philemon					

Figure 14 - Chart by Dr. Rick Yohn

When the young church was birthed in Jerusalem on the Day of Pentecost, it already had a Bible. We call it the Old Testament. This was the very Book from which Jesus and the Apostles quoted time after time. The so-called New Testament was not yet written. That was not written until somewhere around 45-48 A.D. Jesus had died and was resurrected about 33 A.D. And it took several centuries before most of the church recognized the books that the Holy Spirit deemed worthy of being the inspired works of God through men who were committed to get the story out to the nations. We'll begin with Paul's letters. I'm going to use the subdivisions that are found in an excellent small commentary on the New Testament by Dr. Paul N. Benware[1]. He divides the Pauline Epistles into four groups: (1) Paul's Early Epistles; (2) Paul's Major Epistles; (3) Paul's Prison Epistles; and (4) Paul's Pastoral Epistles.

---

1. Paul N. Benware. Survey of The New Testament: (Chicago: Moody Publishers. 1990).

PAUL'S EARLY LETTERS

LETTER	DATE – A.D.	WRITTEN FROM
Galatians	48	Antioch of Syria
1 Thessalonians	51	Corinth
2 Thessalonians	51	Corinth

Galatians – Salvation By Faith & Freedom In Christ

The Galatians began their Christian life with a bang, but soon reverted to the comfort of living life the old fashion way – under the Law of Moses. We can find the location of Galatia on the map of Paul's Second Missionary Journey, found in the chapter on Acts.

Several of Paul's letters are encouraging, but not this one. Listen to some of the statements Paul made to this young church:

"I am astonished that you are so quickly deserting the one who called you by the grace of Christ and are turning to a different gospel – which is really no gospel at all" (Galatians 1:6).

"You foolish Galatians! Who has bewitched you? Before your very eyes Jesus Christ was clearly portrayed as crucified. I would like to learn just one thing from you: Did you receive the Spirit by observing the law, or by believing what you heard? Are you so foolish? After beginning with the Spirit, are you now trying to attain your goal by human effort?" (Galatians 3:1-3)

Paul's emphasis through this letter is our freedom in Christ and man's justification by faith. What do I mean by "justification"? It is a legal term and means "to be declared righteous". The Galatians were attempting to be righteous by their own works – keeping the Law of Moses. The Apostle Paul was reminding them that righteousness does not come by keeping the Law, but rather by faith in the finished work of Jesus on the cross for their sins.

1 & 2 Thessalonians – The Return Of The Lord

Talk about a contrast. Paul's two letters to the believers in Thessalonica couldn't be more different in tone. Paul's first letter is one of tremendous encouragement to believers who were young in the faith and needed some clarification on what Paul had taught earlier, when he was with them. We can find Thessalonica in Macedonia on Paul's Second Missionary Journey map.

The subject matter of both letters focused on the Lord's Return. Apparently, some other teachers of the Word were telling these young believers that those who died would miss out on the Lord's Return for His people. Therefore, the Apostle wanted to clarify that the dead will not miss out on the Lord's Return. He wrote, *"Brothers, we do not want you to be ignorant about those who fall asleep; or to grieve like the rest of men, who have no hope"* *(1 Thessalonians 4:13)*. The Apostle then continues to inform them that the Lord will come in the air and receive both the dead and the living at the same time. The dead in Christ will rise first. *"After that, we who are still alive and are left will be caught up together with them in the clouds to meet the Lord in the air. And so we will be with the Lord forever"* (1 Thessalonians 4:17).

There are several interpretations of this passage. Some say that once we are all caught up to meet the Lord in the air, we immediately return to the earth for Christ to set up His kingdom on earth. Another view is that once this event takes place, we immediately go into eternity with the Lord. One other perspective is that this is the *"Rapture"* of the Church. Believers dead and alive will meet the Lord in the air and will be with Him wherever He is. In the meantime, the people left behind will experience a seven-year period of tribulation on the earth. Jesus spoke about that time as a time of *". . . great distress, unequaled from the beginning of the world until now – and never to be equaled again"* (Matthew 24;21).

However, these young believers had other questions about Jesus' return and needed further clarification. Therefore, the Apostle wrote a second letter to them. He wrote, *"Concerning the coming of our Lord Jesus Christ and our being gathered to him, we ask you, brothers, not to become easily unsettled or alarmed by some prophecy, report or letter supposed to have come from us, saying that the day of the Lord has already come"* (2 Thessalonians 2:1-2). The Apostle then goes into further detail about the Antichrist and the Day of the Lord.

These two letters are the only letters where there is mention of the coming of the Lord in every chapter but one. And Paul looks at Jesus' return as not something to fear, but rather something to anticipate and for which believers should be prepared.

PAUL'S MAJOR LETTERS

LETTER	DATE	WRITTEN FROM
1 Corinthians	54/56	Ephesus
2 Corinthians	55/56	Macedonia
Romans	55/56	Corinth

Figure 15 - Chart by Dr. Rick Yohn

1 & 2 Corinthians – Letters To A Troubled Church (Understanding Sanctification)

Paul's letters to the Thessalonian believers were for clarification and encouragement. However, his letters to the church at Corinth focused on various problems and issues that had arisen since his time in that city. They had experienced salvation, but they needed some understanding about *"sanctification"*, being set apart from the world system and becoming more like Christ Jesus.

One of the first problems that Paul addressed was the divisions within the church body itself. Some of the believers were followers of Peter. Others said that they belonged to Apollos. Then there were those who determined to follow Paul, while the "spiritual ones" said they belonged to Christ. The result? The church was split into four factions.

Another issue arose. A man was sleeping with his father's wife. For the average Corinthian, this was not a moral issue. But for the believer, it was betraying the very type of lifestyle that Jesus wanted His followers to enjoy. Paul had to remind his readers, *"Do you not know that your body is a temple of the Holy Spirit, who is in you, whom you have received from God? You are not your own; you were bought with a price. Therefore, honor God with your body"* (1 Corinthians 6:19-20).

However, during all the problems, the Apostle focuses on one key character quality that could solve many of their problems – **LOVE.**

1 Corinthians 13 is one of the best descriptions of what true love is. It is the type of love that God has for all of us and the same kind of love that He wants us to express to one another. If

Figure 16- Photo by Dr. Rick Yohn
(Acro Corinth & Main Street in Corinth)

we are to understand love from God's perspective, this is a must-read chapter.

And what about his second letter to this congregation? He begins this chapter with a word of comfort and then goes on to talk about his own experiences of hardship. But then he reminds his readers that our focus needs to be on that which is eternal and not on the temporal. And before he completes his letter, Paul challenges them to examine themselves to see whether they are in the faith. He says, *". . . test yourselves. Do you not realize that Christ Jesus is in you – unless, of course, you fail the test"* (2 Corinthians 13:5).

Romans – Righteousness By Faith

This is the Book that radically changed the lives of two very well-known men of the Church and tens of thousands of others over the centuries. The first man is the one we call St. Augustine. Earlier in his life, Augustine determined to live life with no authority over him, spending his time on alcohol, women and whatever else he could find for pleasure. And then one day he came across the following words – *"And do this, understanding the present time. The hour has come for you to wake up from your slumber, because our salvation is nearer now than when we first believed. The night is nearly over; the day is almost here. So, let us put aside the deeds of darkness and put on the armor of light"* (Romans 13:11-12). Those few verses changed Augustine from a prodigal to one of the greatest theologians and defenders of the faith of all time.

Another man experienced a similar change. However, he was neither a womanizer nor an alcoholic. He was a man of the cloth; a priest in good standing in the Roman Catholic Church. But then he came across a passage of Scripture that confounded him for several years. He was always trying to gain God's favor by keeping the rules of the church. But one day he read these words: *"For in the gospel a righteousness from God is revealed, a righteousness that is by faith from first to last, just as it is written: 'The righteous will live by faith'"* (Romans 1:17). What did the Apostle Paul mean when he said, *"The righteous will live by faith"*? This priest suddenly realized that his good works were not going to get him or anyone else to heaven. He came to accept the fact that God declares a man righteous when that person places his faith in what Jesus Christ did for him at the cross, and not on what man does for himself. This priest was changed so radically that he began a movement that would change the course of history. His name was Martin Luther and the movement is known as The Reformation.

The Book of Romans is the Apostle Paul's letter of all letters. It is the mother-lode for doctrine and theology and contains the *"meat of the Word"*. It can be divided into two major sections: (1) Doctrine (chapters 1-11) and (2) Practice (chapters 12-16). In the first eight chapters, the Apostle informs his readers that they are sinners because of Adam's sin and their sin results in death (eternal separation from God, as well as physical death). But Jesus Christ has made it possible for mankind to experience a personal relationship with God, but that relationship can only be established by faith.

Paul then spends three chapters on the nation of Israel and God's plan for her throughout the ages and into the future. Paul raises the following question, *"I ask then: Did God reject his people? By no means! I am an Israelite myself, a descendant of Abraham, from the tribe of Benjamin. God did not reject his people, whom he foreknew..."* (Romans 11:1-2). Later in the same chapter the Apostle raises a similar question about Israel, *"Again I ask: Did they stumble so as to fall beyond recovery? Not at all! Rather, because of their transgression, salvation has come to the Gentiles to make Israel envious"* (Romans 11:11). In other words, God is not finished with the nation of Israel and will one day put His Spirit into their hearts so that they will come to recognize their Messiah, Jesus Christ.

The Apostle then closes out this glorious epistle (chapters 12-16) by showing how to live the Christian life. He writes, *"Therefore, I urge you, brothers in view of God's mercy to offer your bodies as living sacrifices, holy and pleasing to God – this is your spiritual act of worship. Do not conform any longer to the pattern of this world, but be transformed by the renewing of your mind. Then you will be able to test and approve what God's will is – his good, pleasing and perfect will"* (Romans 12:1-2).

PAUL'S PRISON LETTERS

Ephesians	61 A.D.	Rome
Colossians	61 A.D.	Rome
Philemon	61 A.D.	Rome
Philippians	62 A.D.	Rome

Figure 17 - Chart by Dr. Rick Yohn

Why do we call these four Prison Epistles? Each of these four letters was written by the Apostle Paul when he was imprisoned in

Rome. Fortunately, the Apostle was under house arrest and could have visitors. Various believers came to see him both to learn from him and to encourage him. How do we know he was in prison? Listen to Paul's own words as he writes to the believers in Philippi:

"Now I want you to know, brothers, that what has happened to me has really served to advance the gospel. As a result, it has become clear throughout the whole palace guard and to everyone else that I am in chains for Christ" (Philippians 1:12-13).

"Greet all the saints in Christ Jesus. The brothers who are with me send greetings. All the saints send you greetings, especially those who belong to Caesar's household" (Philippians 4:21-22).

As Paul sits in prison, chained to guards, realize that the guards are also chained to Paul. The Apostle had a captive audience. It was contact like this that led to the Gospel penetrating Caesar's household, as one guard after another placed his faith in Jesus Christ. The first letter we'll consider is the one sent to Ephesus.

Ephesians – Life In The Body Of Christ

Ephesus is the first of the seven churches mentioned in the Book of Revelation (Revelation 2:1). It was a church that God blessed with sound doctrine. John the Apostle was one of the pastors to that congregation. In fact, as John sat exiled on the isle of Patmos, he wrote Jesus' following words to this congregation – *"I know your deeds, your hard work and your perseverance. I know that you cannot tolerate wicked men, that you have tested those who claim to be apostles but are not, and have found them false. You have persevered and have endured hardships for my name, and have not grown weary"* (Revelation 2:2-3). What an encouraging word to hear from the lips of the Lord!

**Figure 18 - Photo by Dr. Rick Yohn – The Library of Celsus
in Ephesus**

Paul makes certain that his readers recognized that they all were once "dead" in their sins, but God made them alive with Christ and seated them with him in the heavenly realms. Then the Apostle gets down to some real practical issues and encourages them to *"live a life worthy of the calling you have received"* (4:1); *"no longer live as the Gentiles do, in the futility of their thinking"* (4:17); *"live a life of love"* (5:1); *"live as children of the light"* (5:8) and finally, *"Be very careful, then, how you live – not as unwise but as wise, making the most of every opportunity, because the days are evil"* (Ephesians 5:15-16).

Colossians – Christ In You

Several years ago, I was on a trip to Turkey to visit the seven churches of Asia Minor to whom John wrote in Revelation 2-3. As we were driving through the Western part of the country, I was following a map that our guide was using. I noticed the name Colossae and inquired whether this is the Colossae of the Bible. He replied that it was, so I told him to ask the bus driver to take us there.

Figure 19- Photo by Dr. Rick Yohn – The farmer's sheep pen with Greek inscriptions on the inside of large stones.

We made our way to what was supposedly the city and discovered a farmer's field. I climbed the hill and to my amazement, I discovered numerous stones with carved Greek words in them. Then we visited a farmer's wife and I noticed that the sheep pen was made of the same stones. I asked the lady where she got the stones and she told me from up on the hill (Colossae), I thought to myself, *"Why doesn't the Turkish government begin to excavate some of the many treasures?"* At my feet were superb archaeological treasures just sitting on top of a hill in a farmer's field.

The city of Colossae was also in Asia Minor. Paul placed a major emphasis on the identity of Jesus Christ in this passage. He wrote the following description of the man from Galilee – *"He is the image of the invisible God, the firstborn over all creation. For by him all things were created: things in heaven and on earth, visible and invisible, whether thrones or powers or rulers or authorities; all these were created by him and for him. He is before all things, and in him all things hold together"* (Colossians 1:15-17).

The Apostle also spends time encouraging the believer to put off the old self and to put on the new self. This is an active decision on the part of the believer. God doesn't do it for us. Finally, Paul spells out specific ways to conduct our lives toward one another, directives for husbands and wives, parents and children, and finally, masters and servants (employers and employees).

Philemon – A Slave Gets A Second Chance

This is one of the smallest Epistles in the Bible. It is only 25 verses in length, but is probably the most personal letter throughout Scripture. Onesimus was a slave owner. Philemon was the slave who ran away from his master. He apparently went to Rome, where he caught up with the Apostle Paul, who influenced him to the point of giving his heart to the Lord. Now it was time to send Onesimus back to his owner, but how do you do that? This Book provides a wonderful illustration of what one can do when under the influence of the Holy Spirit.

The Apostle appeals to Philemon to receive his runaway slave, not as a slave, but as a brother in Christ. He then states that if this slave, Onesimus, owes Philemon anything, Paul would pick up the tab. This demonstrated Paul's confidence in Onesimus as a true believer and in Philemon as a gracious and merciful Christian.

Philippians – Rejoice No Matter What Your Circumstances

The city of Philippi, like Thessalonica, was in Macedonia. A business woman named Lydia lived there and came to faith under Paul's ministry (Acts 16:14-15). It was also in Philippi where Paul and Silas were thrown into prison, resulting in an earthquake and the Philippian jailer and his entire household coming to faith in Christ (Acts 16:16-40).

With that as a background, the church in Philippi was established and began to grow. As Paul sat in a Roman prison, his mind probably reflected on the time when he and Silas were in a prison at Philippi. He also most likely thought about the generosity of Lydia and others in that city who supported him in his ministry. It's no wonder that Paul began his letter by thanking them for their *"partnership"* in the gospel from the first day until now (Philippians 1:4). Knowing that they were concerned about his health and potential death, he wanted them to know his attitude towards the future. Therefore, he penned these powerful words – *"I am torn between the two: I desire to depart and be with Christ, which is better by far, but it is more necessary for you that I remain in the body"* (Philippians 1:23-24). He then pivots to one of the greatest descriptions of Jesus' person and work (Philippians 2:5-11). He presented Christ as both God and man to whom every knee will bow and every tongue will confess that Jesus Christ is Lord.

Paul then completes his letter by telling the believers in Philippi to rejoice in the Lord always. Though the Apostle languishes in prison, he wants his friends to rejoice. And then Paul closes the way he began. He thanked them once again for their support of his ministry and assured them that God will meet all their needs based upon his glorious riches in Christ Jesus (Philippians 4:19).

PAUL'S PASTORAL LETTERS

LETTER	DATE	WRITTEN FROM
1 Timothy	62	Macedonia
Titus	63	Ephesus
2 Timothy	64	Rome

Figure 20 - Chart by Dr. Rick Yohn

1 Timothy - How To Pastor A Church

These letters complete the four groups of Paul's Epistles and are directed to two men in charge of specific groups of believers in a specific location. We would call them pastors today. Both were young and needed instruction on how to organize and function as an elder or pastor in a local congregation of believers. Therefore, the Apostle focused on issues such as what appropriate worship was all about and then turned to the two major offices within a congregation, as well as the qualifications for each office (1 Timothy 3).

Timothy is introduced in Acts 16 and was most likely a convert of the Apostle when Paul was on his second missionary journey through Lystra and Derbe (two cities in present day Eastern Turkey). Timothy, like Luke, was a companion of Paul and he is mentioned throughout the New Testament. He was with the Apostle when Paul wrote 1&2 Corinthians, Philippians, Colossians, 1&2 Thessalonians and Philemon.

Timothy was both young and timid, so Paul had to confront him on both issues. He wrote, *"Don't let anyone look down on you because you are young, but set an example for the believers in speech, in life, in love, in faith and in purity"* (1Timothy 4:12)

Titus – Finish What You Started

While Timothy is mentioned in the Bible twenty-five times, you'll read about Titus fourteen times in Scripture, and that is not limited to this Epistle. He is also found in 2 Corinthians, Galatians and 2 Timothy. Like Timothy, this pastor was also a companion of the Apostle Paul.

What did Paul think of Titus? Let's allow him to tell us with these words, *"As for **Titus**, he is my partner and co-worker among you; as for our brothers, they are representatives of the churches and an honor to Christ"*. (2 Corinthians 8:23). In another passage, Paul writes, *"To **Titus**, my true son in our common faith"* (Titus 1:4)

Paul left Titus in Crete so that he could straighten out what was left unfinished and appoint elders in every town (Titus 1:5). Paul then proceeds to inform Titus how to minister with a body of believers when dealing with older men, older women, young men, younger women, slaves and masters. And then he completes his letter by reminding Titus of the Gospel's significance and to focus on it rather than foolish controversies, genealogies, arguments and quarrels about the Law of Moses. He then closes by telling Titus that the believers under his care should *"devote themselves to doing what is good, in order that they may provide for daily necessities and not live unproductive lives"* (Titus 3:14).

2 Timothy – Pass It On To Reliable Men Who Can Teach Others

In his second letter to Timothy, the Apostle continues to challenge and encourage the young pastor. He tells him to fan into flame the gift of God, which is in him through the laying on of hands (2 Timothy 1:6). This is a repeat of what Paul told Timothy in his first letter when he wrote, *"Until I come, devote yourself to the public reading of Scripture, to preaching and to teaching. Do not neglect your gift, which was given youthrough a prophetic message when the body of elders laid their hands on you"* (1 Timothy 4:14).

The Apostle continues to challenge and encourage young Timothy, reminding him that he is in a battle, now that God has entrusted a significant position and responsibility to him. Paul designs a plan for Timothy for a successful ministry. He writes, *"And in the things you have heard me say in the presence of many witnesses entrust to reliable men who will also be qualified to teach others"* (2 Timothy 2:2). This is known as a *"ministry of multiplication"*. Timothy is to train a group of men who will then train others, who will train others, etc.

SIDE BAR: It was Dr. Howard Hendricks (Prof) that used to say, *"Every man should have a Paul, a Barnabas, and a Timothy. He needs a Paul to mentor him, a Barnabas to come alongside and encourage him, and a Timothy whom he can mentor."* Prof Hendricks was my **"Paul"**. He discipled me through my four years at Dallas Seminary and then continually kept in touch with me when I was serving in various churches. Eventually I had the privilege to be his Pastor when I served the church in which he was a member.

Yesterday, I was cleaning up in the basement and I came across some correspondence between myself and Prof. He always had my interest, but never minced words. In fact, a few weeks before I graduated from seminary, I went into Prof's office and asked him to evaluate my qualifications for the new ministry I had accepted. He looked at me and said, *"Yohn, if I were a betting man and you were a horse, I'd put two dollars on you and sweat the whole time you went around the track!"* Not exactly what I was expecting. When I asked him what he meant by his comment, he said, *"You love to begin new projects, but you don't always finish them. You need to learn how to finish what you begin."*

Did I feel a little hurt? Not really, because in my mind I determined from that day forward I would always complete whatever I started, and I can say that I probably have a 95% batting average in that area. I needed a swift kick in the pants and Prof obliged me. And whenever he was in town to speak, whether in the states or in Canada, during my first pastoral ministry, he always stopped by to encourage me.

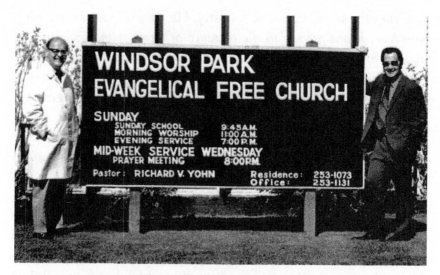

Figure 21 - Prof Hendricks came to visit me in my first pastorate in Winnipeg,
Manitoba, Canada – 1968 (Photo taken by Linda Yohn)

And when I resigned from a difficult situation in one of my churches, he was there to come along side me, pray with Linda and me and then graciously recommended me to whatever ministry the Lord would open. Out of all the professors I've ever had, Prof Hendricks made the greatest impact on my life, and I had the privilege of sharing that with him a few years before he heard his Savior say, *"Well done, good and faithful servant"*.

Paul also informs Timothy that ministry is not a cakewalk. It is a war zone, for Timothy is fighting a spiritual battle like the rest of us. To counter these issues, Paul unveils three scenarios for Timothy and each one includes hardship. Ministry is like a **soldier** who does not get distracted by civilian things, but rather determines to please his master in everything. Furthermore, an **athlete** competes according to the rules. If not, he will be penalized and could be disqualified. And then there is the **farmer** who receives the first of the crops. Each of these positions is one of discipline, faithfulness and eventual reward. So is the ministry.

One of the most often quoted passages of 2 Timothy is found in the third chapter. It deals with the inspiration of Scripture. However, the average person normally stops at verse 16 and misses out on the purpose of why God has given us Scripture. Let's see what both verses say. *"All Scripture is God-breathed and is useful for teaching, rebuking, correcting and training in righteousness, so that the man of God may be thoroughly equipped for every good work"* (2 Timothy 3:16-17).

Not only is the Bible inspired by God, but it is also **"useful"** in four distinct ways: (1) Useful for **teaching** (instructing people in the understanding of the Scriptures); (2) Useful for **rebuking** (most people don't mind the teaching, but often rebel against the rebuking). To rebuke is to let someone know that their words, behavior, manner, behavior or attitude is wrong and needs to be corrected. (3) Useful for **correction**. Rebuke points out the problem while correction provides a solution to the problem – *"This is how you can do it differently next time"*. And then (4) useful for **training in righteousness**. That quality does not come easily for most of us. We are not born righteous. Instead, we enter this world with a sinful nature. That is why we first need teaching, rebuking and correcting. Once those objectives are met, we are prepared to be trained by someone who knows what he/she is talking about. While teaching provides the *"what"*, training shows us *how* to put that knowledge and wisdom into practice.

Paul then answers the great question of **"So What"?** What's the purpose of the Bible? The Apostle answers that question by writing, *"so that the man of God may be thoroughly equipped for every good work"* (2 Timothy 3:17). Every believer needs to be equipped with knowledge, wisdom, motivation, a plan of action and the essential tools for success. The Scriptures provide all of that.

This completes the three Pastoral Epistles and now it is time to learn about the remaining eight letters sent to believers. We call them the General Epistles.

THE GENERAL LETTERS

LETTER	DATE (A.D.)	WRITTEN FROM
James	45	Jerusalem
Hebrews	65	(Unknown)
1 Peter	65	Rome
2 Peter	67	Rome
Jude	70s	(Unknown)
1 John	85	Ephesus
2 John	90	Ephesus
3 John	90	Ephesus

Figure 22 - Chart by Dr. Rick Yohn

James – True Faith Can Be Identified by One's Works

This is probably the first of the Epistles in the New Testament. It precedes the other General Epistles by twenty years and the Book of Galatians by three years. The style is direct and to the point. James was the half- brother of Jesus and after our Lord's death and resurrection, James came to believe that his brother truly was the awaited Messiah. In fact, we are told that after Jesus had appeared to Mary Magdalene, He then appeared to Peter, and then to the Twelve. After that, he appeared to more than five hundred of the brothers at the same time, most of whom were still living, though some had died. Then he appeared to

James. That's when this half-brother came to faith and James soon became the head of the Church in Jerusalem. He was the first one that everybody wanted to hear, because his wisdom and insight mattered (Acts 15:13-21).

James was writing to *"the twelve tribes scattered among the nations"* (James 1:2). This is often called the *"Diaspora"*, referring to those who have dispersed from their home area. Here it is probably referring to Jewish believers living outside of Palestine of that day.

This Apostle points out to his readers that temptation comes from within rather than from God. We are the source of our own temptations (James 1:13-15). He also focuses on demonstrating our faith by our works. Salvation is by faith, but true faith will show evidence that it is for real (James 1:19-27). James then precedes to cut to the chase and expose the hypocrisy in many congregations (James 2). He then moves on to man's foot-in-mouth problem and the two sources of wisdom (God and the devil).

But James continues with his pithy statements and zeroes in on covetousness, friendship with the world, dealing with the devil, slandering others and boasting about tomorrow. It's like a "POW, POW, POW"!!! Finally, James concludes by warning his readers not to oppress the poor, be patient in suffering and pray for the sick. This man lived with his Savior as he was growing up in the same home, though he didn't know it. But after James came to faith in Christ, he was willing to die for his Savior. It is believed that James faced death by first being thrown from the Pinnacle of the Temple and then clubbed to death.

Hebrews – Jesus Our High Priest

This is the only New Testament Book for which we are not certain of the author. Some say it was the Apostle Paul. Others believe it was written by Barnabas or Apollos. Whoever wrote it knew the Old Testament and Judaism extremely well.

- The author identifies with his audience on several occasions. He writes, "*We must pay more careful attention, therefore, to what we have heard, so that we do not drift away*" (2:1). And throughout this Epistle, the author uses the phrase "*Let us*" thirteen times (4:1,11,14,16; 6:1; 10:22, 23, 24; 12:1,28; 13:13,15,18). His audience is probably composed of Jewish believers who knew the Old Testament worship system well, but it appears that they had stopped growing in their Christian faith.

Therefore, the writer first rebukes his readers and then encourages them. He writes, "*In fact, though by this time you ought to be teachers, you need someone to teach you the elementary truths of God's word all over again. You need milk, not solid food! Anyone who lives on milk, being still an infant, is not acquainted with the teaching about righteousness. But solid food is for the mature, who by constant use have trained themselves to distinguish good from evil*" (Hebrews 5:12-14).

In other words, spiritual maturity is the result of believers who are self-starters and get into the Scriptures for themselves. They are like the believers in a town called Berea. The Apostle writes about them when he states, "*Now the **Berean** Jews were of more noble character than those in Thessalonica, for they received the message with great eagerness and examined the Scriptures every day to see if what Paul said was true*" (Acts 17:11).

The author's focus is on the Levitical System (revealed in the Book of Leviticus), with its sacrifices, priests, Levites and Tabernacle. And throughout the entire Epistle, a general theme emerges – Jesus Christ Is Better Than (fill in the blank). For instance, He is **better than the Old Testament Prophets** for He is both the Creator and is the *"radiance of God's glory and the exact representation of his being, sustaining all things by his powerful word"* (1:1-3). He is **better than the Angels** for they are merely God's messenger, but Jesus is God's messenger, but Jesus is God's Son (1:4-2:18). Jesus is **better than Moses**, and worthy of greater honor than Moses, for Moses was a faithful servant of God, but Jesus is a faithful son over God's house (3:1-19).

Furthermore, **Jesus is better than Joshua**, who took the people into the Promised Land and gave them their inheritance that God promised to Abraham. However, as I mentioned earlier, all but two of the first generation that came out of Egypt died in the wilderness and never saw the Land. Furthermore, once they took the Land given them by God, they did not drive out all their enemies. And one more thing – the rest that Joshua gave was temporal, but the rest that Jesus gives is eternal (3:1-4:16).

The author than moves to his next comparison and states that Jesus is **better than Aaron**. Who was Aaron? He was the brother of Moses and God's chosen High Priest for those forty years when the Israelites wandered through the barren desert. However, Aaron was Israel's high priest for a limited time. When he shed blood for the sins of the people, he also had to shed blood for his own sins. But our High Priest, Jesus Christ, is not a priest from the Aaronic Priesthood (those in the blood line of Aaron and his father Levi). Jesus came from the tribe of Judah and is a permanent, eternal High Priest after the order of Melchizedek, a priest revealed in Genesis 14 and to whom Abraham paid tithes. And when He offered up Himself as a sin offering, He used His own blood and not that of bulls and goats. Furthermore, Aaron had to offer up sacrifices day after day, while Jesus offered up Himself once and for all. And since He was sinless, Jesus did not have to offer any sacrifice for His own sins (5:1-12:29).

I find this Book to be one of the most informative Books on the Old Testament sacrificial system. And through it all, Jesus comes out on top: Better than the Old Testament **Prophets**; better than the **angels**; better than **Moses**; better than **Joshua** and better than **Aaron**.

1 Peter – Encouragement Through Suffering

The author of this Epistle is the Apostle Peter who was writing *"to God's elect, strangers in the world, scattered throughout Pontus, Galatia, Cappadocia, Asia and Bithynia. . ."* (1Peter 1:1). This was the disciple who denied Jesus three times. He was the one who bragged, *"I'll never fall away!"* (Matthew 26:33). He was the disciple who was privileged to see Jesus' transfiguration as He stood talking with Moses and Elijah (Acts 18). But that was then and this is now.

He knew how miserably he had failed the Lord. But now having experienced the forgiveness of His Savior, Peter was prepared to minister and encourage others. Peter, like many of us came to realize that God is the God of second opportunities. He picks us up, brushes us off and sends us on our way.

Peter was writing to believers who were experiencing various types of suffering, possibly due to the general Roman population in which they lived. *"Everyone"* seemed to be worshipping the many gods of the Greeks and Romans, except for these *"Christians"* who believed in one God and His Son Jesus Christ. Peter is providing a Biblical worldview of suffering when he writes, *"These (trials) have come so that your faith – of greater worth than gold, which perishes even though refined by fire – may be proved genuine and may result in praise, glory and honor when Jesus Christ is revealed"* (1 Peter 1:7).

Peter encourages his readers to grow in their faith when he writes, *"Like newborn babies, crave pure spiritual milk, so that by it you may grow up in your salvation, not that you have tasted that the Lord is good" (1 Peter 2:2).* And for any of these believers who were feeling emotionally and physically drained, he informs them who they truly are in Jesus Christ. He writes, *"But you are a chosen people, a royal priesthood, a holy nation, a people belonging to God, that you may declare the praises of him who called you out of darkness into his wonderful light"* (1Peter 2:9).

Peter then focuses on specific groups of people such as Servants and Masters, Wives and Husbands, and then *"all of you, live in harmony with one another"* (4:8). And the one who was totally unprepared to stand up for Christ after the Lord's arrest now challenges his readers to always be prepared to give an answer to everyone who asks them to give a reason for the hope they have (3:15). The word translated *"give an answer"* is the Greek word from which we derive our tem *"apologetic"*. This does not mean that we apologize for our faith, but that we are prepared to *"defend"* our faith. In other words, we know what we believe and why we believe it.

Peter then closes by directing his readers' attention to walk with humility, recognizing that the devil prowls around like a roaring lion looking for someone to devour. And to deal with the devil is not to fight him, for he knows each of us better than we know ourselves. Peter's formula for defeating the devil is *"humble yourselves, therefore, under God's mighty hand, that he may lift you up in due time" (1Peter 5:6).* Then once we humble ourselves before

God, we are then prepared to resist the devil by standing firm in the faith (1 Peter 5:6-9).

2 Peter – Proper Conduct Is the Result of Knowing the Truth

When Peter wrote this letter, he knew that his readers were facing false teachers who had crept into their assemblies and distorted God's Word. Like the devil in the garden, they would sow seeds of doubt, such as, *"Did God really say . . ."* (Genesis 3:1).

Peter addressed the problem by stating at the outset that the believers needed to add several very important ingredients to their faith such as goodness, knowledge, self-control, perseverance, godliness, brotherly kindness and love. He then concludes with his opening remarks by writing," For *if you possess these qualities in increasing measure, they will keep you from being ineffective and unproductive in your knowledge of our Lord Jesus Christ"* (2 Peter 1:5-9).

The Apostle knew that his days were numbered (2 Peter 1:13-15) and wanted to make certain that his readers' faith was based upon the truth of God's Word. Therefore, he approached them with an appeal to remind them of truth he was assuming they already knew – *"So I will always remind you of these things, even though you know them and are firmly established in the truth you now have"* (2 Peter 1:12).

He then informed his readers of the origin of the Scriptures. The Word of God did not originate with man, but rather with God Himself. He says, *"For prophecy never had its origin in the will of man, but men spoke from God as they were carried along by the Holy Spirit"* (2 Peter 1:21). From this statement, he lets them know of the motivation and fate of these false teachers. Peter reminds them that God did not spare the angels who sinned against Him, nor the ancient world when they rebelled against Him, or the cities of Sodom and Gomorrah. He knows how to hold the unrighteous for the day of judgment while continuing their punishment (2 Peter 2).

Finally, Peter ends his letter with a view towards the future, including the Second Coming of Jesus Christ. There were many scoffers in his day who denied that Jesus was going to return. And Peter addressed the time issue by writing, *"But do not forget this one thing, dear friends: With the Lord a day is like a thousand years, and a thousand years are like a day. The Lord is not slow in keeping his promise, as some understand slowness. He is patient with you, not wanting anyone to perish, but everyone to come to repentance"* (2 Peter 3:10).

What a great insight into the heart of God! Yes, there is a heaven and there is a Hell. God's heart's desire is for all men and women to repent of their sins and seek His forgiveness. And yet He is aware that many people on earth will have no interest in Him until it is too late.

This might be a good time for reflection. If you have any questions about your own relationship with Jesus Christ, you can remove all doubt at this very moment. If you have not already acknowledged that you have sinned against God and need His forgiveness, this would be an excellent time to put down this book and spend some time with the Creator of all things. He is the One who loves you and has made it possible for you to spend eternity with Him and to experience everything in this life for which He has created and gifted you.

Jude – A Defense for the Faith

Jude states that he had planned to write to his readers about the salvation they share, but then felt compelled to write and urge them to contend for the faith that was once for all entrusted to the saints – *"Dear friends, although I was very eager to write to you about the salvation we share, I felt I had to write and urge you to contend for the faith that was once for all entrusted to the saints"* (Jude 1:3).

I mentioned in the 1 Peter section that the word translated *"give an answer"* (1 Peter 3:15) is the Greek word from which we derive our tem *"apologetic"*. Well the letter from Jude is an apologetic, a defense for the faith. It is short (one page), but powerful.

In many ways Jude sounds like 2 Peter as he expounds on God's judgment on the first generation of Israelites He brought out of Egypt due to their unbelief. He likewise expounds on the angels who rebelled against Him, and His judgment on Sodom and Gomorrah. Jude then applies such judgment to those false teachers who have infiltrated newly established churches.

Jude then calls his readers to persevere in their faith by building themselves up in their faith and praying in the Holy Spirit, as well as by showing mercy to others. He then closes out his letter with a beautiful blessing – *"To him who is able to keep you from falling and to present you before his glorious presence without fault and with great joy – to the only God our Savior be glory, majesty, power and authority, through Jesus Christ our Lord, before all ages, now and forevermore! Amen"* (Jude 1:24).

1 John – The Believer's Fellowship with the Father & Son

The Apostle John wrote the Gospel of John, 1,2,3 John and Revelation. Here we will capture the essence of his first letter. We should keep in mind that this writer was a disciple of the Lord and had the privilege of observing Him day after day for three years. Therefore, he reminds his readers that they are hearing from one who knew the Lord intimately, face to face.

The word *"fellowship"* is found four times in this Epistle. John writes, *"We proclaim to you what we have seen and heard, so that you also may have **fellowship** with us. And our **fellowship** is with the Father and with his Son, Jesus Christ. . . If we claim to have **fellowship** with him yet walk in the darkness, we lie and do not live by the truth. But if we walk in the light, as he is in the light, we have **fellowship** with one another, and the blood of Jesus, his Son, purifies us from all sin"* (1 John 1:3,6-7).

The most common phrase used in this Epistle is ***"we know"*** and it is found 19 times in these five chapters. There was a group of individuals known as *"Gnostics"* who believed that they had superior knowledge, a secret knowledge that others did not possess. John therefore addresses their teachings by reminding his readers of the certainty that we have in Christ.

We know:

> That we have come to know him (2:3)
> We are in him (2:5)
> It is the last hour (2:18)
> When he appears, we shall be like him (3:2)
> Who the children of God are and who the children of the devil are (3:10)

We have passed from death to life (3:14)
What love is (3:16)
We belong to the truth (3:19)
He lives in us. by the Spirit he gave us (3:24)
We live in him and he in us (4:13)
And rely on the love God has for us (4:16)
That we love the children of God (5:2)
He hears us when we pray (5:15a)
We have what we asked of him (5:15b)
Anyone born of God does not continue to sin (5:18)
We are children of God, and the whole world is under the control of the evil one (5:19)
The Son of God has come and has given us understanding, so that we may know him who is true (5:20)

One other phrase that John uses quite often in his Epistle (6 times) is **"eternal life"**. The concept of eternal life was so important to John that he devoted an entire Gospel to writing about it. In that Gospel, he told his readers, *"But these are written that you may believe that Jesus is the Christ, the Son of God, and that by believing you may have life in his name"* (John 20:31).

Now in this letter, John once again focuses on life eternal. In fact, John tells us why he has written this Epistle – *"I write these things to you who believe in the name of the son of God so that you may know that you have eternal life"* (1 John 5:13). How can a person know for certain that he does or does not possess eternal life? John makes it easy for us to understand. He tells us, *"And this is the testimony: God has given us eternal life, and this life is in his Son. He who has the Son has life; he who does not have the Son of God does not have life"* (1 John 5:11-12).

If you have received Christ as your Savior, you possess eternal life. If not, eternal life is available, but you can receive it only

on this side of life. Once death claims your body, that option is off
the table. That is why the Apostle Paul wrote, *"I tell you, now is the
time of God's favor, now is the day of salvation"* (2 Corinthians 6:2).

2 John – Walk in Truth & Love

Though his first letter was written to a general audience, John's
second letter is addressed to *"the chosen lady and her children"*.
We are not told who this *"chosen lady"* was, but scholars believe
she probably was some eminent Christian lady.

Once again John is dealing with the false teaching that has
crept into the church. As he addresses this woman, he stresses the
need to walk in obedience to the Lord's commands because many
deceivers, who do not acknowledge Jesus Christ as coming in the
flesh, are going out into the world preaching their heresy. He also
warns her not to invite anyone into her house who denies that
Jesus has come in the flesh. Apparently, this lady's house was the
place where believers met for worship.

The two words that are often used together in this letter
are *"truth and love"*. John tells this lady that he loves her and her
children *"in the truth"* (1:1). He also states that grace, mercy and
peace will be with us in *"truth and love"* (1:3). He then commends
her and her children for *"walking in the truth"* (1:4) and then
encourages her family to also *"walk in love"* (1:6).

3 John – Dealing with Church Conflict

What do we do with conflicts in the church? How should we handle them? John provides us with first-hand experience. The two
weapons at our disposal are *"truth and love"*. Just as his Second

Epistle was addressed to an individual, so was his third Epistle. The receiver of this letter was a man named Gaius, most likely a leader in the church. Apparently, another man was jealous of John and fought for the attention of the congregation. His name was Diotrephes, *"who loves to be first:"*. John lists four issues with this man: (1) He loves to be first; (2) He wants nothing to do with John and those who support him; (3) He refuses to welcome the brothers; and (4) He also stops those who want to do so and puts them out of the church.

In contrast to Diotrephes, another man named Demetrius was well spoken of by everyone – and even by the truth itself. Much like his Second Epistle, John once again emphasizes the twin qualities of truth and love. But truth without love can come across very judgmentally and may be difficult to receive. And love without truth may push the boundaries to make exceptions and degenerate into subjective truth, i.e. what is true for me may not be true for you. Therefore, any conflict needs to be resolved by aligning the issue with the truth of God's Word, but presenting that truth in the spirit of God's love.

10

The Story Completed
(The Book of Revelation)

Out of the sixty-six books of the Bible, none seem to be as controversial as the book of Revelation. And often because it can be controversial, most pastors and Bible teachers refrain from preaching or teaching it. The losers of this refusal are the everyday believers who wonder what the future holds for the world, their families and themselves. And what is interesting is that this is the only book in the entire Bible that promises a blessing to *"the one who reads the words of this prophecy, and blessed are those who hear it and take to heart what is written in it"* (Revelation 1:3). And one of the greatest blessings is to know that, despite all that is going on around us, God is indeed in control and has a great future in store for all those who know Him and live for Him.

Furthermore, this last Book of the Bible completes God's love story to us. In the first chapter of this Book we learn that it is a letter from the One who loves us and dedicated to the One who loves us – *". . . and from Jesus Christ, who is the faithful witness, the firstborn from the dead, and the ruler of the kings of the earth. To him who loves us and has freed us from our sins by his blood, and has made us to be a kingdom and priests to serve his God and Father – to him be glory and power for ever and ever! Amen"* (Revelation 1:5-6)

Controversy and difficulty in understanding should never prevent us from reading and studying any book of the Bible. Refusing to read Revelation is like purchasing a great novel and reading it up to the last chapter and then putting it down and never discovering how it ends. This book tells us how it ends.

Our Approach To Revelation

There are four major approaches to how we should interpret this book. (1) The Preterist (Past) Approach sees this book as having been fulfilled in the First Century; (2) The Idealist Approach considers Revelation as the continual conflict between good and evil; (3) The Historical Approach views Revelation as a narration of church history from the First century to the Second coming of Christ and the last judgment; and (4) The Futurist Approach sees the first three chapters as historical events and then chapters 4-22 as future.

We know that its genre is apocalyptic material. What does that mean? Dr. Elliott Johnson writes, *"Apocalyptic writers spoke to a historic audience during crisis and suffering and gave that audience perspective by stepping above its own day and sharing a vision of the resolution of the conflict at the end of history."*[*] Therefore, when we interpret what John is attempting to tell his first readers of the first century, we need to understand his words from their perspective. However, in most prophetic and apocalyptic literature there is a near and far perspective.

---

* Elliott E. Johnson, *Expository Hermeneutics: An Introduction* (Grand Rapids, MI: Academic Books, Zondervan Publishing House, 1990), p.165.

In other words, statements are made that apply to the time and situation when it was written, but may also be applicable for some time in the future. Therefore, when we approach Revelation, we must consider what the believers of the first century were experiencing, but also realize that this book also has a future perspective, a time when Jesus will return to the earth and take back His rightful throne:

"Look, he is coming with the clouds, and every eye will see him, even those who pierced him; and all the peoples of the earth will mourn because of him. So shall it be! Amen" (1:7)

"He will rule them with an iron scepter; he will dash them to pieces like pottery" (2:27)

"Then I heard every creature in heaven and on earth and under the earth and upon the sea, and all that is in them, singing: 'To him who sits on the throne and to the Lamb be praise and honor and glory and power, for ever and ever!'" (5:13)

"Then they gathered the kings together to the place that in Hebrew is called Armageddon" (16:16)

"He seized the dragon, that ancient serpent, who is the devil, or Satan, and bound him for a thousand years" (20:2).

"Then I saw a new heaven and a new earth, for the first heaven and the first earth had passed away, and there was no longer any sea. I saw the Holy City, the new Jerusalem, coming down out of heaven from God, prepared as a bride beautifully dressed for her husband" (21:1-2).

None of these events can be traced to any historical event in any century. Therefore, they must be future. Based on these facts, we will approach this book from both a historical, as well as a future perspective, using a literal or normal means of interpretation while recognizing the many figures of speech and apocalyptic symbols.

The outline of Revelation can be found in the first chapter: *"Write, therefore, what you have seen, what is now and what will take place later"* (1:19).

1. What you have seen (chapter one)
2. What is now (chapters 2-3)
3. What will take place later (chapters 4-22).

What You Have Seen (Revelation 1)

What did John see? What he saw is described in the first chapter of this book. Though he had seen Jesus many times, he had never seen the Lord like this. Oh, he did capture a unique perspective of the Lord in the Mount of Transfiguration, but this was more intense. The brilliance of the light overwhelmed John. How was he going to describe what he saw? There was nothing on earth with which he could make a comparison, but he made the following attempt.

"I turned around to see the voice that was speaking to me. And when I turned I saw seven golden lampstands, and among the lampstands was someone like a son of man, dressed in a robe reaching down to his feet and with a golden sash around his chest. The hair on his head was white like wool, as white as snow, and his eyes were like blazing fire. His feet were like bronze glowing in a furnace, and his voice was like the sound of rushing waters. In his right hand he held seven stars, and coming out of his mouth was a

sharp, double-edged sword. His face was like the sun shining in all its brilliance" (1:12-16)

Lamp stands, stars and brilliant light shrouding a figure that looked like a man. That's some sight to behold. But what does it all mean? One of the benefits of apocalyptic literature is that at times it interprets itself. This is one of those cases. Later in the chapter we are told that the lamp stands are the seven churches in Asia Minor and the seven stars are the pastors or leaders of those churches (Revelation 1:20). John is told to write to each church and that brings us to the next two chapters.

What Is Now (Revelation 2-3)

The seven churches are real historical churches. I know because I visited all seven locations. If you ever want to go on a learning vacation, I would recommend visiting Ephesus. That is where the first church in Revelation was located. In each of these letters the Lord gives each church a commendation, but then follows it with a reprimand. There are two exceptions to this pattern. The church at Laodicea received no commendation and the church at Smyrna received no reprimand.

Imagine if the Lord sent a letter to your pastor and he read it next Sunday at church. What do you think Jesus would say about your church? We might even ask ourselves for what would he commend us? For what would He reprimand us? Such questions might be revealing if we ask them to our Bible Study group or to our Sunday School class. I am sure we could take up the entire hour if we opened the group to discuss each question.

What will take place later (revelation 4-22)
Heaven's mission control (4-5)

Now we come to the bulk of the Lord's message and John catches a glimpse into the future – our future. In chapters 4-5 John is ushered into heaven itself and captures a vision of God the Father, the Holy Spirit, and the Lord Jesus Christ as never seen previously by the human eye. It is from this Mission Control Center that all of life is governed.

The Father is seated on a throne encircled by an emerald rainbow. The Holy Spirit appears as seven Spirits. Around them are four living creatures that were introduced back in the first chapter of the book of Ezekiel. In addition, twenty-four elders appear in the scene, casting their crowns before God the Father.

John continues to gaze at this amazing vision playing out before him, and suddenly two animals appear on the scene. The first is the Lion of Judah and the second is a lamb that was slain. This lamb takes the scroll of seven seals from the hand of God the Father. As the Lamb receives the scroll from the One on the throne, the four living creatures bow before Him. They are suddenly accompanied by thousands of angels and then ten thousand times ten thousand begin their praise of *"Worthy is the Lamb."*

John is filled with awe and most likely would love to join in and become part of this great worship service. However, that beautiful scene fades and another scene appears as the first of the seven seals is opened by the Lamb

The Tribulation Period (6-18)

This is the largest section of the book of Revelation. The focus is on God's judgment upon all mankind for its rebellion against God, wanting to eliminate Him from their lives. The prophet Joel describes this time as *"The Day of the Lord"*. It is a terrible and dreadful day. There's never been a time like this previously nor will there be any like this in the future and it has been predicted by God's Prophets over the centuries.

The Prophet Isaiah – *"See, the day of the LORD is coming – a cruel day, with wrath and fierce anger – to make the land desolate and destroy the sinners within it. The stars of heaven and their constellations will not show their light. The rising sun will be darkened and the moon will not give its light. I will punish the world for its evil, the wicked for their sins"* (Isaiah 9-11a).

The Prophet Joel – *"The day of the LORD is great; it is dreadful. Who can endure it?"* (Joel 2:11b). *"The sun and moon will be darkened, and the stars no longer shine. The LORD will roar from Zion and thunder from Jerusalem; the earth and the sky will tremble"* (Joel 3:15-16)

Throughout this section there are three consecutive judgments, each series followed by another series more intense and devastating.

First come the seven **Seal Judgments (Revelation 6).**

The first four Seal Judgments include the Four Horsemen of the Apocalypse: (1) White Horse (Conqueror/Antichrist); (2) Red Horse (Removes peace from the earth); (3) Black Horse (Famine); (4) Pale Horse (Death/Hades).

Then the fifth Seal unveils those who are martyred during this period who cry out to the Lord, *"How long, Sovereign Lord,*

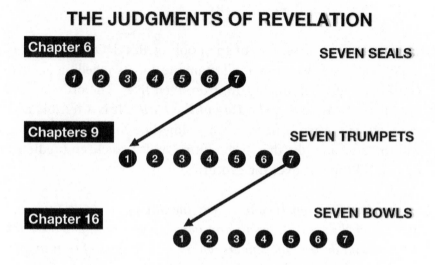

THE JUDGMENTS OF REVELATION

Figure 23 - Chart by Dr. Rick Yohn

holy and true, until you judge the inhabitants of the earth and avenge our blood?" (Revelation 6:10). The sixth Seal results in a great earthquake, followed by other cosmic catastrophes. Finally, the seventh Seal Judgment begins the next series of judgments.

The Seal Judgments are followed by the **seven Trumpet Judgments (Revelation 8-9).** The first judgment results in 1/3 of the vegetation burned, then 1/3 of the sea is judged and 1/3 of fresh water is judged, followed by 1/3 of the moon and stars give no light. The fifth Trumpet Judgment results in an increase of demonic activity, followed by a great invasion from the East. Once again, out of the seventh Trumpet Judgment, the final seven Bowl Judgments emerge.

The **Bowl Judgments (Revelation 16)** are the most devastating of the group. They begin with cancerous sores on men and then the sea turns to blood, followed by the fresh water turning to blood. By the fourth Trumpet Judgment men are scorched with fire and they curse the God of heaven. Then comes a drying of

Figure 24 - From Har Megiddo, looking to the Jezreel Valley (Armageddon).
Photo by Dr. Rick Yohn

the Euphrates River and an invasion by the kings from the East. As these armies come together, they gather at a place called Har Megiddo, or what we call Armageddon.

The final judgment results in such a great earthquake that the great city splits into three parts and the cities in the nations collapse. On top of all that, huge hailstones of about 100 pounds each fall upon men.

No, the world has never seen such universal devastation since the world-wide flood of Noah's day. People often ask, *"Why does God allow terrorists to blow up people, behead them, and burn them alive? Why does He allow children and young girls to be sold into prostitution? Why does He allow so much pain and suffering on the earth? Why doesn't God do something about those who take advantage of others?*

The Bible tells us that God is a loving God and doesn't want anyone to perish and go to Hell. He patiently continues to open His arms to those who are willing to come to Him in repentance. But the day is coming when He will say, *"Enough! I've given mankind many opportunities over the centuries, and now I must judge the sin of man"*. This Tribulation Period is that Judgment.

Besides the four chapters of twenty-one judgments, other events occur during this Tribulation on earth. In chapter seven 144,000 Jewish evangelists preach the Gospel throughout the earth. In chapter eleven two witnesses appear in Jerusalem who have great power to prevent the sky from releasing rain, as well as turn the waters into blood. Eventually they are killed and are raised from the dead three and a half days later and ascend into heaven before the eyes of the world.

In **chapter twelve** we read about a pregnant woman and a dragon. The woman is believed to represent Israel, who gives birth to a son (Jesus). The dragon (Satan) waits to devour the newborn, but the child is snatched up to God and to his throne and the woman flees into the desert, where she is taken care of for 1260 days, which is three and a half years.

In **chapter thirteen** we read about two beasts. One comes up out of the sea and the other comes out of the earth. It is believed that the first beast represents the Antichrist and the second represents his cohort, the False Prophet, who encourages mankind to worship the Antichrist.

And then there are **chapters 17-18** which speak of Babylon. Some see this as a restored Babylon which is outside of present day Baghdad, Iraq. Others believe that the Babylon of chapter 17 represents *"religious"* Babylon and chapter 18 represents *"commercial"* Babylon, both systems and not cities. In other words, the false world religion of the day will be destroyed, as well as the collapse of the world economy.

The Second Coming Of Jesus Christ (Revelation 19)

Then, what was predicted by the prophets of old, as well as Jesus Himself, the heavens open and the Son of Man descends to the earth with the holy angels and with those who have placed their trust in Him.

The Prophet Zechariah states – *"On that day his feet will stand on the Mount of Olives, east of Jerusalem, and the Mount of Olives will be split in two from east to west, forming a great valley, with half of the mountain moving north and half moving south . . . Then the Lord my God will come, and all the holy ones with him. . . The Lord will be king over the whole earth"* (Zechariah 14:4,5,9).

The Prophet Daniel writes – *"In my vision at night I looked and there before me was one like a son of man, coming with the clouds of heaven. He approached the Ancient of Days and was led into his presence. He was given authority, glory and sovereign power; all peoples, nations and men of every language worshiped him. His dominion is an everlasting dominion that will not pass away and his kingdom is one that will never be destroyed"* (Daniel 7:13-14).

Jesus Christ proclaimed – *"Immediately after the distress of those days 'the sun will be darkened, and the moon will not give its light; the stars will fall from the sky, and the heavenly bodies will be shaken.' 'At that time the sign of the Son of Man will appear in the sky, and all the nations of the earth will mourn. They will see the Son of Man coming on the clouds of the sky, with power and* *great glory. And he will send his angels with a loud trumpet call, and they will gather his elect from, the four winds, from one end of the heavens to the other"* (Matthew 24:29-31).

The Apostle John envisioned – *"I saw heaven standing open and there before me was a white horse, who rider is called Faithful and True. With justice he judges and makes war. His eyes are like blazing fire, and on his head are many crowns. He has a name written on him that no one knows but he himself. He is dressed in a robe dipped in blood, and his name is the Word of God. The armies of heaven were following him, riding on white horses and dressed in fine linen, white and clean. Out of his mouth comes a sharp sword with which to strike down the nations. 'He will rule them with an iron scepter.' He treads the winepress of the fury of the wrath of God Almighty. On his robe and on his thigh he has this name written: King of Kings and LORD of LORDS"* (Revelation 19:11-16)

The Milennium (1,000 Year Reign Of Christ) (Revelation 20)

If we continue to interpret this book with a literal (normal) means of interpretation, we will conclude that 1,000 years means 1,000 years. Usually when a term is used again and again in the passage of scripture, the writer is attempting to convey something very important. If you look at the 20th chapter of Revelation, you'll notice that one phrase is used many times. That phrase is **"one-thousand years"** and is presented six times in seven verses. It would seem reasonable to take this in a normal, literal sense.

At the beginning of this time, believers are raised from the dead, Satan is bound for one thousand years and then is released to deceive the nations, who in turn come against Christ and are destroyed by fire. The devil is thrown into the lake of burning sulfur, where the beast and the false prophet had been thrown to be tormented day and night for ever and ever.

The New Heavens And New Earth (Revelation 21-22)

John's final sightings extend to a new heaven and earth. In a sense, it is a "do-over" of God's original creation, that man ruined with sin. The Apostle John sees the Holy City, New Jerusalem, descend from heaven, prepared as a bride. This is when the Lord wipes away all tears, for there is no more death, mourning, crying or pain, as it was in the beginning. John then attempts to describe this New Jerusalem which has no temple, sun or moon, for the glory of God gives it light.

In the final chapter of this tremendous Book, John sees the river of the water of life, flowing from the throne of God and of the Lamb, a reminder of the original Garden of Eden, where *"a river watering the garden flowed from Eden; from there it was separated into four headwaters . . ."*. There will be no more night, for the Lord God will give them light and believers will reign with Christ forever and ever.

This great Book ends with an invitation to all who are willing to hear. *"The Spirit and the bride say, 'Come!' And let him who hears say, 'Come!'. Whoever is thirsty, let him come, and whoever wishes, let him take the free gift of the water of life"* (Revelation 22:17).

If you've never experienced the new birth that our Lord desires for you to enjoy, this is your invitation to come to Him and receive the free gift of salvation. If you know that Jesus Christ is your Savior, this would be a wonderful time to thank Him for what He has stored up for you in the future.

This is where we need to focus when we feel unloved or forgotten, or we are experiencing pain and suffering. Listen to one who experienced much pain, suffering and rejection. He focused on the eternal rather than on the temporal. The Apostle Paul wrote, *"Therefore we do not lose heart. Though outwardly we are wasting away, yet inwardly we are being renewed day by day. For our light and momentary troubles are achieving for us an eternal glory that far outweighs them all. So, we fix our eyes not on what is seen, but on what is unseen. For what is seen is temporary, but what is unseen is eternal"* (2 Corinthians 4:15-18).

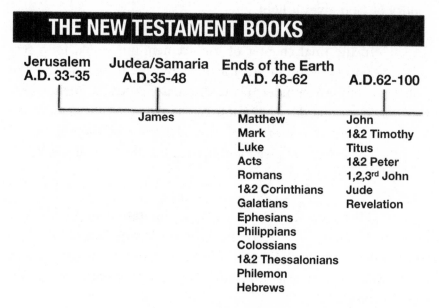

Figure 25 – Chart by Dr. Rick Yohn

11

The Story's Lover

The god so many people imagine is often not the God of the Bible. Too often there is a conflict in our minds between the god we've mentally created and the God who has revealed Himself in Scripture. For instance, we expect that when we live decent and respectable lives, things should go well for us. But when we come down with cancer or lose a loved one or experience a major accident and are laid up for an extended time we wonder where God is. How could He allow such a thing to happen? When bad things happen to good people, we have a choice to make. As I said twice previously, **we will either interpret the situation in the light of what we know about God, or we will interpret God based on the situation.**

I recently attended two memorial services for friends of mine. One man was the President of the University where I had been the Dean of Biblical and Theological Studies and the other was a member of the church I attend and manager of a nearby Chick-Fil-A. He was also the son of missionaries and was married to a lady who also is the child of missionaries. The President of the University was a godly man and my age. The manager was in his prime with a child in high school and another who just graduated from high school. Where was God in all of this?

I'll answer that question through the experience I had at the two memorial services. The Lord was certainly front and center at both services because both men loved and served Him faithfully. The President of the University battled cancer for over ten years, and yet I never heard him complain about his battle or about God. Instead, whenever he would speak at public events, he would repeat his favorite phrase, *"Jesus, Jesus, Jesus!"*.

Likewise, the manager of Chick-Fil-A was an avid, life-long hiker and loved climbing the fourteeners of Colorado. He had been hiking the Colorado Rockies for years without incident. But on this one occasion he lost his footing and fell 400 feet to his death. Yet no one in his family was blaming God. Instead, they realized that he had fallen into the arms of the Savior, whom he loved, and they now look forward to being united with him once again. How could they come to such a conclusion? Because their God is not the god of their imagination, but rather the God of the Bible. Now let's see what God has to say about Himself.

We may ask, *"Why is it so important for us to know the God of the Bible?"* My answer to that question is because **you will either interpret life's circumstances based on your knowledge of God, or you will interpret the Person and character of God based on your circumstances.** If we don't know the God of the Bible and we are making decisions based on a god of our imagination, we may find ourselves blaming God, hating God, rejecting God and possibly make some very poor and costly decisions that could affect the rest of our lives. Therefore, let's begin by learning what God tells us about Himself.

You Will Know Him By His Character

The Lord first made Himself known to Moses on Mt. Sinai. As God passed in front of Moses, He said, *"The LORD, the LORD, the compassionate and gracious God, slow to anger, abounding in love and faithfulness, maintaining love to thousands, and forgiving wickedness, rebellion and sin. Yet he does not leave the guilty unpunished; he punishes the children and their children for the sin of the fathers to the third and fourth generation."* (Exodus 34:6-7)

Let's look at this passage a little more closely. Notice that God first revealed Himself to Moses as a God of mercy, which is one of His many expressions of love. And to demonstrate what He meant by compassionate or merciful, God was about to deliver the Israelites from 430 years of slavery. In other words, God was telling Moses, *"This is who I am, and to show you what I mean by mercy, this is what I'm about to do"*.

COMPASSIONATE/MERCIFUL - The ESV translation records these words as *"merciful and gracious"*. Other translations use the word *"compassionate"*. They are similar, but may be used with a slightly different connotation.

A compassionate individual has pity on those who are hurting and then does something to alleviate the problem. Recall the time when Jesus gave His parable of the Good Samaritan. He first described three men who saw someone lying in the road that went from Jerusalem to Jericho. Two of the three men passed on the other side of the road, while the third man, a despised Samaritan, stopped to help the wounded man. The Lord then asked His listeners, *"Which of these three do you think was a neighbor to the one who fell into the hands of robbers?"* (Luke 10:36). The answer – *"The one who had mercy on him"* (Luke 10:37). Mercy is an *"active"* attribute of an individual's character. Mercy leads to action, to do something that will relieve the misery of another.

And when it comes to God, there is an additional dimension of mercy which He demonstrates. And that is a mercy that *"does not give us what we deserve"*. In other words, it withholds punishment in hope of the offender repenting for what he has done. Because of our sinful nature and our actions, we *"deserve"* God's punishment, just as your children deserve your punishment when they purposely disobey you. But the Psalmist argues, *"The Lord is compassionate and gracious, slow to anger, abounding in love. He will not always accuse, nor will he harbor his anger forever; he does not treat us as our sins deserve or repay us according to our iniquities"* (Psalm 8-10).

God's mercy includes His patience. He puts up with a lot of bad behavior and decisions, waiting for us to recognize how badly we have offended His righteousness and holiness. Though we deserve immediate retribution from God, He shows us mercy time and again. And He is not only merciful. God is also a God of grace.

GRACIOUS - While mercy is not giving us what we do deserve, grace is *"giving us what we do not deserve"*. We don't deserve His patience with us, or His love for us. We don't deserve how He protects us and provides for our needs. The Bible clearly indicates, *"for all have sinned and fall short of the glory of God"* (Romans 3:23). We've failed the test of God's standards and character. That does not mean that we are evil people. It's just means that we do not measure up to the character and standards of God. Therefore, we need to be related to a merciful and gracious God who understands our spiritual and moral weaknesses.

When someone offends us, it's next to impossible to be gracious to them. Our tendency is to think of ways we can retaliate.

And too often, our mouths say things that we are often sorry about later, but the words have already escaped.

Is there another way to respond to those who offend us? Well, we could use God as our model and demonstrate grace. In other words, we continue to treat that individual with respect and show them that, though they treat us badly, we will respond to them with God's love. You may be thinking, *"You've got to be kidding. I've been hurt many times in the past and those people don't deserve my love or respect."* That's true. They don't deserve your love or your respect. But that's where grace comes in the door. Grace treats people, not based on how nice they've been to us, but rather because of our character. When we allow the character of God to make itself known through us, the people who have offended us will experience grace, God's grace. Now let's consider a third wonderful quality of our God.

SLOW TO ANGER – Think about that. How often have we tried God's patience? For years, we live in sin and do everything that our hearts desire, and yet God does not send a lightning bolt to zap us.

When a child enters the world, parents rejoice, take tons of photos and brag about how beautiful their child is. But as time passes and the beautiful child begins to act like the sinner he is, the parents' anger begins to boil. The parent tells the child to stop doing what he is doing, but the child is determined to do what he pleases. Eventually, the parent has had it and anger takes over. He/she is about to teach that child who is in charge and who must obey.

And what about our God? How often have we tried His patience? How many times have we confessed our sins, only to do it all over again? How often have we thought that, even though we know a specific decision is wrong, we are determined to do what we please and violate one Biblical principle after another? Does God immediately get even with us? Does He make life miserable for us until we cry *"Uncle"*? No, He is *"slow to anger"*. But that's not all. Consider a few other qualities of our God's character.

ABOUNDING IN LOVE AND FAITHFULNESS – When Moses was leading the people through the wilderness, they complained that they didn't have any water. In response to the issue, Moses cried out to God and notice the results – *"I will stand there before you by the rock at Horeb. Srike the rock, and water will come out of it for the people to drink,' So Moses did this in the sight of the elders of Israel.'"* (Exodus 17:6). Think about this abundance in these terms. The Israelites numbered about two and a half million people, plus their livestock. How do you provide enough water in the desert for that many people and animals? The only way that can accomplished is by a God who is compassionate, merciful, gracious and abounds in love and faithfulness.

But our Lord is also a God of *"more than enough"*. It was around 1924 when Dallas Theological Seminary was in its infancy and known as *"The Evangelical Theological College"*. The School was experiencing some financial issues and graduation was just around the corner. Based on the following article, God provided "more than enough".

One year several weeks before May graduation, the leaders had a few days to decide whether the school would continue. Three people were awakened at 5 a.m. on a Saturday—Dr. William Anderson, a Dallas pastor instrumental in the Seminary's founding; Dr. Chafer, founder and first president; and a donor. None knew the others were awakened, and each was impressed with the need to pray about the burden the Seminary faced. Only weeks later did they learn that all three had been awakened at the same time. It took the donor about two weeks to get the money ready. And at the time it arrived, Dr. Lewis S. Chafer, Dr. Rollin T. Chafer, Dr. C.

Fred Lincoln, and Dr. Harry Ironside prayed together on a Monday morning in the office. After praying they sat for a few minutes in silence. There came a knock at the door and a government bond for $10,000 arrived from an unknown banker in Illinois.[1]

Today, that amount would be approximately between $135,000 to $140,000. It was enough to cover expenses and more than enough for them to confidently continue the Theological College for the foreseeable future.

God will provide enough when we need just enough and more than enough when we need to meet our present bills, but also need to move into the future in faith. He indeed is *"Jehovah Jireh"*, the God who provides. And when He does provide, He doesn't hand out blessings with a grudging attitude. Think of it in these terms, just as you love to give gifts to your children, especially at Christmas, so does God love to pour out His abundance upon us time and again.

But God's abundance is not merely physical and financial. He also abundantly gives us His love and faithfulness. The God of the Bible is totally dependable. Whatever need you may have at this moment, God can provide. God has no limitations of love and faithfulness. He never runs out of either amazing quality.

And yet, at times we may feel as though God is down on us because of how we feel inside. We know that something is not right between us and God. We may be walking around with a sense of shame, or feel like He is ready to somehow get even with us for something we did in the past. This is called *"guilt"*. Sometimes the guilt is well-deserved, while at other times it is a false guilt. By that I mean we may feel guilty about not measuring up to

---

1. Bailey, Mark and Yarbrough, Mark. *"Kindred Spirit"*. Autumn, 2014. (p.3-4).

someone else's standard or the standard of a local church or group of other believers, though we may measure up to God's standard. That's false guilt. But let's look at true guilt. We know that we've sinned against God and haven't dealt with that sin. Therefore, we are waiting for that punishment of God to hit us hard sometime soon. Well, I've got good news.

HE WILL NOT ALWAYS ACCUSE – Have you ever been accused of something that you never did? Joseph had that experience in Biblical times, when he was falsely accused of the rape of his boss' wife, that resulted in a long prison sentence (Genesis 39). Jesus was accused of blasphemy and spent hours on a cross until he gave up His spirit.

It can be a tough situation when you are accused of something that you didn't do, but it is even worse when you are accused of something you did. Some of our Presidents, Vice Presidents, Congressmen, presidents of TV networks, business executives, stock brokers, teachers, coaches, clergy and others in major positions have had to face charges that were true and many of them paid a great price for their actions.

Sometimes a friend makes accusations against us. Other times it may be someone we have hurt by our words, actions or even deeds of omission. Then there are those times we are accused by people who just don't like us. But what about those *"inner"* accusations? You know, the ones that eat at you from the inside. That feeling of guilt. The hope that no one will ever find out.

Those feelings may be coming from the Holy Spirit who is convicting us of something we've said or done. When He convicts us of our wrong doing, it is so we will admit our sin and confess it to the Lord, and experience His fellowship again. Or it may be coming from the *"accuser of the brothers and sisters"*

(Revelation 12:10). I'm referring to the Devil. He continues to tell us that we are not good enough. That we've failed God again. That we are not deserving of God's forgiveness. He accuses us day and night. But the good news is that we have an advocate (Lawyer) with the Father, Jesus Christ. And when the Devil accuses us before the Father, our *"lawyer"*, Jesus Christ tells the Father, *"I've died for that sin"*. When the Holy Spirit convicts us of sin and we confess it before God, there is no more accusation.

MAINTAINING LOVE . . . FORGIVING – Forgiveness emerges from love. God can forgive us only because of His love for us. Even when our children rebel against us, they are still our children. We may become angry at them and want to immediately punish them, but then love takes over. They are still our children. We love them because of who they are and whose they are, not because of their behavior. We are more prepared to forgive those who belong to us than we are to forgive those with whom we have no relationship.

The sweetest sound any one of us can hear, after we've hurt someone is *"I forgive you"*. People forgive us out of love and not because we deserve their forgiveness. Likewise, God forgives us because of who we are and because of whose we are. We belong to Him. We are His family. We are children of God. He will discipline us when we get out of hand, but His love demands forgiveness and we are the recipients of that abounding love.

A wonderful demonstration of that love was expressed in the last words of our Savior as He hung on the cross, *"Father, forgive them, for they do not know what they are doing"* (Luke 23:34). The Lord could have prayed, *"Father, give them what they deserve!"* You may wonder how Christ could have prayed these words at such a time. But let's think about ourselves. What does the Bible tell us about God's love for us? Paul captures God's love when he writes,

"But God demonstrates his own love for us in this: While we were still sinners, Christ died for us" (Romans 5:8). Christ did not wait until we improved our spiritual and moral condition. He didn't wait until we were better. He demonstrated His love for us while we were in rebellion against Him and wanted nothing to do with Him.

It's wonderful to know how God deals with us, but let me raise an important question. How often do we display that same kind of love to others? Jesus taught His disciples to pray, *"Forgive us our debts, as we also have forgiven our debtors"* (Matthew 6:12). Note the *"as we have forgiven"*. We ask Him to forgive us based on our willingness to forgive others who have hurt us. And when we refuse to do that, we are telling God, *"I deserve your forgiveness for what I've done to you, but that person doesn't deserve my forgiveness for what he/she has done to me."* Really? We don't deserve God's forgiveness, nor does that person deserve our forgiveness.

The concept of forgiving one another is never based on *"deserve"*. Rather, it is based on love, mercy and grace, all qualities of our God. But does that mean we can sin as much as we want? Not at all! The Apostle Paul addressed that issue when he wrote, *"What shall we say, then? Shall we go on sinning so that grace may increase? By no means! We died to sin; how can we live in it any longer?"* (Romans 6:1-2) When we do sin, there is a way to deal with it. The Apostle John tells us, *"If we claim to be without sin we deceive ourselves and the truth is not in us. If we confess our sins, he is faithful and just and will forgive us our sins and purify us from all unrighteousness. If we claim we have not sinned, we make him out to be a liar and his word has no place in our lives"* (1John 1:8-10). First, we must admit to ourselves that we have sinned against God and then we confess (agree with God) that we have sinned. He will then faithfully forgive us, recognizing that as a *"just"* God, He has already dealt with our sin at the cross by placing His Son there as our substitute. Forgiveness is always available, but when we continue in sin and refuse to acknowledge what we are doing, God will deal with us.

DOES NOT LEAVE THE GUILTY UNPUNISHED – Many people believe that God will never punish sin. Listen to these words from the Psalmist who writes about the arrogant man, *"God has forgotten; he covers his face and never sees"* (Psalm 10:11). And then he raises this question, recognizing the stupidity of such a thought, *"Why does he say to himself, 'He won't call me to account'"* (Psalm 10:13)? Truthfully, the Lord does see our actions and He has not forgotten. When we confess our sins, God will quickly forgive. But when we harbor sin in our lives and refuse to deal with it on God's terms, God will deal with our sin in His time and based on His terms.

Sometimes we become impatient with God when we know that someone deserves to be zapped by Him, and yet it seems that individual has gotten away with it. It doesn't look as though he is being punished at all. But God's delay is not the same as God's denial. He will deal with the sinner, but also be gracious to the one who repents (turns away from) of his sin.

We've looked at a handful of verses that give us a sneak peak of some of those wonderful and awesome attributes of God. But let's add another means of understanding a little more of our Creator. Consider the names that He had revealed about Himself.

God is known by his names
What's in a name?

Most of us have been named by our parents to honor a family member, or some famous individual. For instance, my grandfather's name was **Martin Van Buren Yohn**. Though many people today have no idea who Martin Van Buren was, he was the eighth President of the United States. I have no idea why my great-grandparents would name their son after a President who was blamed for the Depression that followed the Panic of 1837, but that's where my grandfather received his name. However, pieces of that name flowed down to the next three generations. My grandparents named my Dad, Henry **Martin** Yohn. And then my parents held on to one more smidgen of the name and named me Richard **Van** Yohn. My wife and I named our first-born son after me. And when you think about it, what difference does it make? Are names that important? Perhaps not as much today, but when you look at some of the names by which God has made Himself known to us, you discover that He is telling us something about Himself.

Elohim - The first introduction we have about God is found in Genesis 1:1 – *"In the beginning God created the heavens and the earth"*. The Hebrew name is *"Elohim"* and means *"to swear"*. In other words, when God makes a promise, He keeps His promise because He *"swears"* on the oath of His name and character that He will follow through. The Book of Hebrews informs us that *"Men swear by someone greater than themselves, and the oath confirms what is said and puts an end to all argument. Because God wanted to make the unchanging nature of his purpose very clear to the heirs of what was promised, he confirmed it with an oath. God did this so that, by two unchangeable things in which it is impossible for God to lie, we who have fled to take hold of the hope offered to us may be greatly encouraged"* (Hebrews 6:16-18). First, God confirms His promise with an oath (which puts an end to all arguments) and then He confirms it with His character – it is impossible for God to lie.

Today in courts around the country, people swear in the name of God. When our Presidents are sworn into office, they put their right hands on the Bible and swear by the Bible that they will uphold the U.S. Constitution. In doing this, they are saying that what is in the Bible is superior to them and they place themselves under the authority of the Bible. At least, that is what was originally expected. I'm afraid that today, too many of our government officials swear by the Bible and then make laws and decisions based on what they think is best, even when it conflicts directly with the teachings of Scripture. But that's another subject all together. We want to focus on the faithfulness of God. He cannot and will not do anything that is contrary to His nature.

El – *"The Strong One"*. Whenever this name is used in a compound form, strength and might connect with it. It can also be translated as *"Mighty"*, *"First in Prominence"*. In other words, there is nothing higher, greater or more powerful. Now let's look at how the name "El" is used in a compound form.

El Elyon – *"The Most-High God"*. This was the name by which God made Himself known to Abraham, when this patriarch met a priest named Melchizedek, who blessed Abraham with the following blessing – *"Blessed by Abram by God Most-High, Creator of heaven and earth. And blessed be God Most High, who delivered your enemies into your hand"* (Genesis 14:19). The concept of *"Most-High"* means that there is nothing *"higher"*, *"loftier"* or *"stronger"* than God. Nothing can compare with Him. He alone is God. He spoke to His people through the Prophet Isaiah by reminding them, *"Remember this, fix it in mind, take it to heart, you rebels. Remember the former things, those of long ago; I am God, and there is no other; I am God, and there is none like me. I make known the end from the beginning, from ancient times, what is still to come. I say: 'My purpose will stand, and I will do all that I please'"* (Isaiah 46:9-10).

You may be wondering, *"What about the Muslim god Allah? And what about the gods of Shintoism and Hinduism?"* Well, you'll have to decide at this point. Either God is true when He says, *"there is no other God"* or He is a liar. If He is true in what He says, then Allah and the other gods do not exist. They are only gods in the imaginations of those who worship them. You often hear people say that we all worship the same God. It's just that we each give Him a different name. Really? If that is the case, then this god whom we all worship contradicts himself time and again.

Hindus don't believe in heaven and the Muslim way to heaven differs greatly from the Biblical way to heaven. All other religions are based on a *"merit system"*. In other words, there are certain works that you must perform before God will accept you into heaven. But the Scriptures teach a different means of salvation. Jesus Christ did the *"merit"* for us. He died in our place. He paid the penalty for our sin. We do nothing to get to heaven other than receive the gift of grace that God offers to us. *"For it is by grace you have been saved, through faith – and this not from yourselves, it is the gift of God – not by works, so that no one can boast"* (Ephesians 2:8-9).

Furthermore, because we live in a pluralistic and politically correct society, we are told not to say anything against someone else's beliefs. That might be society's standards, but it certainly wasn't Jesus' standard. He was completely politically incorrect when He made the statement, *"I am the way and the truth and the life. No one comes to the Father except through me"* (John 14:6).

You may question, *"Does that mean that Jesus is the only way to heaven? What about the Muslim way and the way of other religions?"* What about them? Do they also say that Jesus is the only way to God the Father? No. Jesus was either telling the truth or He was a liar or just delusional. That's a decision we all must make ourselves. And if we believe that there are other ways to God, then we cannot say that Jesus was a good man, because good men don't go around deceiving.

Let's add one more thing about *"not offending"* another person's religion. Most people think that Jesus was at least a good man. He was the poster child for love, patience, goodness, mercy, etc. Well listen how this *"good"* man confronted the religious leaders of His day – *"Woe to you, teachers of the law and Pharisees, you hypocrites! You shut the kingdom of heaven in men's faces. You yourselves do not enter, nor will you let those enter who are trying to. 'Woe to you, teachers of the law and Pharisees, you hypocrites! You travel over land and sea to win a single convert, and when he becomes one you make him twice as much a son of hell as you are. 'Woe to you, blind guides! . . . '"* (Matthew 23:13-16). He later adds, *"You snakes! You brood of vipers! How will you escape being condemned to hell?"* (Matthew 23:33).

Loving? Yes, He was. And Jesus is also just and righteous in judging between good and evil, as well as between truth and fiction. God is the Most High and Jesus is the Son of the Most High. There is none higher, more righteous, more just and more deserving of our worship. It is true that we should love and accept one another, but God expects us to use discernment between truth and error. We cannot demand that others accept what we believe, but we must discern people's truth claims with what the Scriptures teach.

EL ELOAH – This is the singular form of Elohim and means *"The Everlasting or Eternal God"*. *"Abraham planted a tamarisk tree in Beersheba, and there he called upon the name of the Lord, "the Eternal God"*. What can we learn from this name? We discover that God had neither a beginning nor does He have an ending. He always was and always will be. That concept goes beyond our ability to comprehend.

Each of us has had a time of birth and we all have a time of death. But El Eloah is not like man. He always existed. That means that no event or being came before Him and nothing will outlast Him. Therefore, God knows us so well. He saw each one of us emerge from our mother's womb and He will see us when our soul departs from our bodies. He knows us perfectly: our thoughts, our actions, and our omissions. He has always been and He will always be. And for those of us who have some years behind us, it's hard to imagine someone who never grows old. He does not become weaker as the years pass. He is just as able today as He was when He created the heavens and the earth. He is the *"everlasting"* God. And He is also the God who has no needs.

EL SHADDAI – *"The All-Sufficient One", "God Almighty".* God does not need our help, our counsel, or our efforts to accomplish anything. He doesn't need our gifts, our money, or anything that we could offer Him. He never gets into trouble. He never runs out of anything, whether it be grace, mercy, thoughts, ideas, love, etc. Remember that He is the God of *"abundance"*. And He loves to share His never-ending supply with each one of us.

El reminds us that He is mighty and powerful. And Shaddai focuses on His sufficiency. He informed His people years ago, *"I have no need of a bull from your stall or of goats from your pens, for every animal of the forest is mine, and the cattle on a thousand hills. I know every bird in the mountains, and the creatures of the field are mine. If I were hungry I would not tell you, for the world is mine, and all that is in it"* (Psalms 50:9-12). And yet, God includes us in His plans and involves us in carrying out ministries that He has planned long ago.

Not only does He include us, but He has also gifted us so that we can be effective in serving and ministering to one another. Paul writes about this wonderful fact by saying, *"Now to each one the manifestation of the Spirit is given for the common good"* (1Corinthinans 12:7). And when he writes to the believers in Rome, he says, *"We have different gifts, according to the grace given us. If a man's gift is prophesying, let him use it in proportion to his faith. If it is serving, let him serve; if it is teaching, let him teach; if it is encouraging, let him encourage; if it is contributing to the needs of others, let him give generously; if it is leadership, let him govern diligently; if it is showing mercy, let him do it cheerfully"* (Romans 12:6-8). No, God does not *"need"* us to do His work, but He is pleased to invite us to join with Him in carrying out His work. Though there are other compound names beginning with El, let's consider another set of compound names.

Though Moses was a Hebrew, he was bought up Egyptian. He spoke the language of Egypt, was reared in Egyptian culture, thought like an Egyptian, and for all intense and purpose, He was Egyptian. However, he never forgot the things his mother taught him when she was still with Him. So, when Moses saw that burning bush, and a voice began to speak to him from that bush, Moses had to ask God, *"What's your name?"* Moses knew about the Hebrew God, but did not know Him intimately, not even His Name. On that very day, Moses began his Theology 101 Class.

Jehovah – God introduced Himself with a very special name. We say Jehovah, but it is more like Yahweh. The name comes from the Hebrew verb *"to be"*. God told Moses, *"I AM WHO I AM"* (Genesis 3:14). Then God added these words, *"This is my name forever, the name by which I am to be remembered from generation to generation"* (Genesis 3:15). God was, is and will be. He is the self-existing God with neither beginning nor end. He is dependent on no one, needs no one's counsel, and does as He pleases.

The Prophet Isaiah, speaking on behalf of God, raised the following questions to his readers, *"Who has understood the mind of the Lord, or instructed him as his counselor? Whom did the Lord consult to enlighten him, and who taught him the right way?"* (Isaiah 40:13-14) And then he adds, *"Before me no god was formed, nor will there be one after me. I, even I, am the Lord, and apart from me there is no savior. I have revealed and saved and proclaimed – I, and not some foreign god among you"* (Isaiah 43:10-12)

And though God does not need my counsel or my input, He does say, *"Come now, let us reason together"* (Isaiah 1:18). He loves conversation. He loves to establish a relationship with us and meet with us each day. He wants to hear from us and then make Himself known more to us through His Word. We don't have to be concerned that He will somehow forget a promise or fail to carry through on a promise.

We don't have to worry that He might someday disappear and never return. He is Jehovah, the Promise Keeper or Covenant Keeping God. He is the God who is concerned about your needs. Listen to how Jehovah expressed Himself to Moses concerning His people who lived in slavery: *"I have indeed **seen** the misery of my people in Egypt. I have **heard** them crying out because of their slave drivers, and I am **concerned** about their suffering. So, I have come down to **rescue** them from the hand of the Egyptians and to bring them up out of that land into a good and spacious land. . ."* (Exodus 3:7-8). I love these four special verbs: God **sees** our need. God **hears** our prayers. God is **concerned** when we are being mistreated. God is willing to **rescue** us from our dilemma. All of that is wonderful, but our Lord adds other modifiers to His name of Jehovah.

Jehovah-Jireh – This name was revealed to Abraham after God told him to take his son Isaac to Mount Moriah and offer him as a sacrifice to God. Abraham obeyed completely. When Isaac told his father that he had the wood and the fire, he was wondering about the lamb for the sacrifice. Abraham replied that God would provide the lamb (Genesis 22:7-8). And just when Abraham was about to plunge the knife into his only son an angel told him to stop. As Abraham slowly lowered his knife, he heard the bleating of a ram, caught in the thickets. Abraham saw this as a sign and a provision of God. The ram was God's substitute for Isaac. Abraham's response to what God had done for him was to name the place Jehovah Jireh, *"the Lord will provide"*. My wife and I have seen this fleshed out in our lives many times over the years. God is our Provider. And He is also the God of Peace.

Jehovah-Shalom – *"The Lord is Peace"*. This name comes from the days of the Book of Judges. One of the Judges was named Gideon. When God called Gideon to fight against an enemy much greater than he, Gideon needed some type of sign from God. So, God allowed him two signs and told him to go out and fight the Midianites, a war-like people who were harassing Israel. God also promised him that he would not die. So, Gideon built an altar to the Lord and gave the altar a name – Jehovah-Shalom (The Lord Is Peace) (Judges 6:24).

Many battles that we fight within ourselves are battles against the Lord. We want to do something that we know in our hearts and mind is against what God wants from us. We continue to justify our decision in our minds, but guilt continues to surface in our emotions. Finally, like the Prodigal, we come to our senses, and return to our Father. At that very moment, we experience the peace of God that is beyond comprehension. Our battle is over. Our mind is at rest. We feel good all over again.

Or perhaps we may be going through a very difficult period in life where God seems to have disappeared. It may be a great loss, a sense of failure, or a decision with which we've been struggling for some time. But as we continue to rest in the Lord, the fog begins to dissipate and we see things more clearly than ever before. At that moment, the emotional turmoil begins to lift and is replaced by the peace that comes from one Source only – the God of Peace, Jehovah – Shalom.

Here's God's promise to us about peace: *"Do not be anxious about anything, but in everything, by prayer and petition, with thanksgiving, present your requests to God. And the peace of God, which transcends all understanding, will guard your hearts and your minds in Christ Jesus"* (Philippians 4:6-7).

Finally, let's consider a few other amazing qualities about this God of the Bible. We will look at what He knows, the decisions He makes, His ability, availability and dependability.

God Is Known By His Attributes (Qualities)

There are theological ways to identify the various qualities of God and then there are everyday adjectives that you can ascribe to Him. I'll use both approaches, beginning with the everyday descriptions. We'll begin with a Psalm that was written by King David.

God Knows It All (Omniscience)

"O Lord, you have searched me and you know me. You know when I sit and when I rise; you perceive my thoughts from afar. You discern my going out and my lying down; you are familiar with all my ways. Before a word is on my tongue you know it completely, O Lord. You hem me in – behind and before; you have laid your hand upon me. Such knowledge is too wonderful for me too lofty for me to attain." (Psalm 139:1-6)

The Lord *"searches"* each one of us. The Hebrew word means *"to investigate"*, *"to explore"*, *"to examine"*. We are not always comfortable with that concept. There are things in our lives that we would just as well be pleased if no one found out what we were thinking, feeling or even doing. But God knows our thoughts and actions because He explores even our motives – *"All a man's ways seem innocent to him, but motives are weighed by the Lord"* (Proverbs 16:2). Ouch! That can be a little convicting, can't it? There are times when we do good things, but we do so with selfish motives. Perhaps we are looking for name recognition. Or maybe we expect some future advancement. Our maybe it's because we just want people to notice how spiritual we are. And many times, we don't even know our motives. But God knows.

He also knows when we get up and when we lie down, as well as everything in between. He even knows what we are going to say before we say it. The Hebrew word translated *"know"* means *"to perceive"*, *"to recognize"*. It means that God has full understanding about us. His understanding is not faulty whatsoever. He knows us perfectly. His knowledge of us is quite different from our knowledge of one another.

God's knowledge about us is perfect. We cannot deceive Him. We cannot pretend before Him. We cannot make excuses and say that we didn't mean to do this or that. He knows us far better than we even know ourselves. Let's discover more about God as we continue reading this great Psalm 139.

God Is Always Here (Omnipresence)

"Where can I go from your Spirit? Where can I flee from your presence? If I go up to the heavens, you are there; if I make my bed in the depths, you are there. If I rise on the wings of the dawn, If I settle on the far side of the sea, even there your hand will guide me, your

right hand will hold me fast. If I say, 'Surely the darkness will hide me and the light become night around me,' even the darkness will not be dark to you; the night will shine like the day, for darkness is as light to you" (Psalm 139:7-12).

Wherever we are, God is there. We can't hide from Him and when we turn out the lights, He can see our actions as though it were a bright, sunny day. There is nothing that God cannot see, because He is present when we are living life wherever we are living life. For many people this truth is very encouraging, while for others, it is quite disconcerting, uncomfortable.

The times when I've been in a foreign country, surrounded by a language I didn't know and customs that were unfamiliar, I was glad to remember that God was right there with me to help me navigate through the differences of language, custom and geography. Likewise, when we are in an uncomfortable situation and feel all alone, we should recall the words of the Psalmist when he says, *". . . even there your hand will guide me, your right hand will hold me fast."* Those words should be a great comfort to us. Now let's look at God's great and awesome power.

God Is Able (Omnipotence)

"For you created my inmost being, you knit me together in my mother's womb. I praise you because I am fearfully and wonderfully made; your works are wonderful; I know that full well. My frame was not hidden from you when I was made in the secret place, When I was woven together in the depths of the earth, your eyes saw my unformed body. All the days ordained for me were written in your book before one of them came to be" (Psalm 139:13-16).

It is God who formed us in our mother's womb. And as the sperm and egg met and all the cells began their formation, God saw it all. Today we can see this beautiful process develop, but this Psalm was written three thousand years ago. No man had the ability to watch the miraculous process of *"formation"*. However, David was confident that God saw it all many years ago.

David adds one more caveat in this passage when He speaks about all the days God has ordained for each one of us. When each of us enters this world, we are on a time clock. However, none of us knows the days that have been numbered. This information is in God's mind alone. However, the Bible does tell us to number our days ourselves. Listen to this prayer of Moses when he writes, *"The length of our days is seventy years – or eighty, if we have the strength; yet their span is but trouble and sorrow, for they quickly pass, and we fly away . . . Teach us to number our days aright, that we may gain a heart of wisdom"* (Psalm 90:10,12).

When I was young, health never crossed my mind. I did what I wanted to do when I wanted to do it. I recall the days on the high school swimming team. When we practiced, the coach had us swim lap after lap. I enjoyed that immensely because I would sing to myself in my mind and make my strokes to coincide with the rhythm of my songs. Sometimes I'd swim for an hour or more, and that never bothered me. The energy was always available. And it was the same with jogging. Whether I was running three miles, six miles or fifteen miles, there was no issue. The energy was always there. It was just a matter of my discipline and will. However, today things are different. By the time this book is in print, I'll have turned 80 years old. How could such a young, energetic individual ever get saddled with age? That was just for those *"old people"*, not me.

Yes, I'd love to swim for an hour or go out and jog three to six miles, but my body tells me, *"There's no way that I'm going to cooperate with you. You might as well accept your age and just go for a walk"*. Now I'm taking the advice of Moses and I number my days, wanting every day to count for something. When the Lord informs me that *"Today is the day to come home"*, I want know that I've done everything in my power to honor Him in my life and that I've also shared with my family, friends, and with those I've never met what He has taught me over the years. That's why I'm writing this book; to inform my readers that this is a love story from God that can change their lives forever.

Let's look at one more awesome quality of our God. The theologians call it *"sovereignty"*.

GOD IS SOVEREIGN – For most of us, this is a foreign term. The United States was formed as the result of rebelling against one who saw himself as *"sovereign,"* levying heavy taxes on a people who had no representation in the government. Because of this history, we have no King in the White House. Instead, we have a representative government of three branches so that there would be *"checks and balances"* in the government.

By the way, this concept of three branches of government is derived from the Book of Isaiah where we read, *"For the Lord is our Judge (judicial branch), the Lord is our lawgiver (legislative branch), the Lord is our king (executive branch); it is he who will save us"* (Isaiah 33:22). Since God is righteous and just, He is our sovereign, our King. He makes the rules (legislative); enforces the rules (executive); and when they are violated, He judges the violators (judicial). That covers all three branches of a Holy Government. But since man is sinful and separated from God, we need checks and balances in our own government.

As our Sovereign, God does what is in our best interest and what pleases Him. Listen to some of the aspects of what a

Sovereign does. Listen to the testimony of another *"sovereign"*, King Nebuchadnezzar. He was the ruthless king who invaded Jerusalem three times. In 605 B.C., he removed many of the young men from Jerusalem and took them back to Babylon. One such young man was Daniel. Then in 597 B.C. Nebuchadnezzar invaded the city again and took out more people to Babylon, including a man named Ezekiel. And finally, in 586 B.C. the king destroyed Jerusalem and the temple of Solomon.

But one day the king had a dream and invited the prophet Daniel to interpret for him. Daniel boldly informed the king that his dream had come from the God of heaven and earth, and that he needed to repent of his sins or else he would be driven away like a mad man for seven years until he recognized the Sovereignty of heaven.

Nebuchadnezzar refused the words of Daniel and eventually went insane for seven years. Then one day he came to his senses and here is his testimony: *"At the end of that time, I, Nebuchadnezzar, raised my eyes toward heaven, and my sanity was restored. Then I praised the Most- High; I honored and glorified him who lives forever. His dominion is an eternal dominion; his kingdom endures from generation to generation. All the peoples of the earth are regarded as nothing. He does as he pleases with the powers of heaven and the peoples of the earth. No one can hold back his hand or say to him: 'What have you done?' . . . Now I, Nebuchadnezzar, praise and exalt and glorify the King of heaven, because everything he does is right and all his ways are just. And those who walk in pride he is able to humble"* (Daniel 4:34-35, 37). What does all this mean?

1. **It means that we can plan our ways, but God decides on the outcome** – *"In his heart a man plans his course, but the Lord determines his steps"* (Proverbs 16:9). *Many are the plans in*

a man's heart, but it is the Lord's purpose that prevails" (Proverbs 19:21). *"A man's steps are directed by the Lord. How then can anyone understand his own way?"* (Proverbs 20:24). *"There is no wisdom, no insight, no plan that can succeed against the Lord"* (Proverbs 21:30).

I've always loved to set goals and then draw up the methods I had planned to use to reach those goals. Then I would look over my chart to monitor the progress. Sometimes I would be successful and at other times issues arose that prevented me from reaching my goals.

Recently I have been downsizing and getting rid of a lot of stuff that we've accumulated over our 57 years of marriage. I've thrown away my radio tapes and sermons on reel to reel tapes. I've given my library to a good friend who is going to seminary and whom I know God will use greatly in the future. I'm also digitizing thousands of photos, because I plan to throw away most of the hard copies. And in the process of all of this, I've looked through old correspondence and read about books that I never started and others that I never completed. I've read about opportunities that sounded great at the time, but something interfered with either accepting or getting very far into the opportunity. And though I made many plans over the years, God had the last say in the matter. Sometimes it was *"Yes, move ahead and you'll be successful"*; sometimes *"not now, but perhaps later"*; and sometimes, *"No, this is not what I have planned for you"*. Of course, we don't know those answers until we invest the time and energy to attempt the challenge.

2. **It means that God will use difficult circumstances in our lives for our own good.** Even though Joseph was sold into slavery by his brothers and though they hated him and wanted to kill him, God gave him the opportunity to tell them later in life,

"You intended to harm me, but God intended it for good" (Exodus 50:20). *"And we know that in all things God works for the good of those who love him, who have been called according to his purpose."* (Romans 8:28).

None of us wants to experience bad times, but we do. And when we go through those difficult experiences, we can become more bitter towards God or more committed to Him. If we allow our circumstances to frame our concept of God, we will probably become more bitter towards Him. But if we allow the Bible's revelation of God's character to frame our concept of God, we will most likely become more committed to Him.

Concerning those tough times, the Apostle Paul informs us that *". . . we also rejoice in our sufferings, because we know that suffering produces perseverance; perseverance, character; and character, hope"* (Romans 5:3-4). Those difficult experiences of life can lead us to a humbler and godly character.

3. **It means that God is never caught by surprise.** Though we are often surprised by our circumstances, God knows the beginning from the end because He is the Sovereign who planned the future of mankind. He tells us, *"I foretold the former things long ago, my mouth announced them and I made them known; then suddenly I acted, and they came to pass. . . Therefore, I told you these things long ago; before they happened I announced them to you so that you could not say, 'My idols did them; my wooden image and metal god ordained them'"* (Isaiah 48:3,5).

4. **It means that God's ways are very different from our ways and His thoughts different from our thoughts** – Job was confused because he led a very good life, but was experiencing horrible results. He did the right things and then lost everything.

It didn't make any sense. His experience contradicted everything that he thought about God. And yet, while still confused, Job held to his faith. Though he couldn't believe it, he accepted it. And in the end, he came to understand that God doesn't play by our rules or grade us on a curve. The Bible makes it clear that we think at a level that prevents us from fully understanding why God does what He does or why He allows bad things to happen to good people. The Prophet Isaiah spoke these words for God, *"For my thoughts are not your thoughts, neither are your ways my ways, declares the Lord. As the heavens are higher than the earth, so are my ways higher than your ways and my thoughts than your thoughts"* (Isaiah 55:8-9).

5. **It means that you and I are not in control of life, God is.** Too often we attempt to help God out. Abraham experienced that lack of faith when he had a child with Hagar, named Ishmael. God promised him a son and time passed. Sarah was becoming frustrated waiting for a pregnancy in her old age, so she encouraged her husband to have a child with her handmaid, Hagar. Eventually Abraham and Sarah had the joy of welcoming God's promised child into the world and named him Isaac. We don't realize that whatever we possess and control can be taken from us in an instant. Job had it all, and in a short time, it was all gone. Moses was a prince, brought up in the royal family of an Egyptian Pharaoh. But one bad decision and act of murder changed his life forever. His fame, prestige, position and future heir of the throne went up in flames in a moment. And for the next forty years, Moses was a fugitive and lowly shepherd, having fallen from ruling over people to herding a flock of sheep.

We may think, *"But I have nothing to fear because I have plenty of money in my portfolio. I'm safe for the rest of my life."* Listen to the wisdom of Solomon on this matter. *"Do not wear yourself out to get rich; have the wisdom to show restraint. Cast but a glance at riches, and they are gone, for they will surely sprout wings and fly off to the sky like an eagle"* (Proverbs 23:4-5). Whether you have a lot of money, a great job, wonderful health, or anything else that you may be taking for granted, it can all disappear quickly. That's why God is your refuge and a very present help in time of trouble. Confidence in anything else that you may possess is futile.

Now let's see where you fit into this picture. Do you interpret life's events by your knowledge of the God of the Bible, or do you interpret God by the circumstances around you and in the world? Whatever your answer, let's be sure you know the kind of God the Bible presents.

He is compassionate and gracious, merciful, slow to anger and quick to forgive and yet does not let the guilty off the hook. He abounds in love and faithfulness. He is the strong, most-high God. There is none like Him, nor will there ever be any like Him. He is everlasting, without a beginning or end. He is all sufficient in Himself and is all sufficient for you and me. Whatever we need, He can supply.

He is our promise-keeper, our provider and our peace. God knows us better than we know ourselves. There is no knowledge that exists of which He is unaware. He is always with us, wherever we are, and He can meet whatever need we have. And He is the sovereign God, which means that He determines the outcome of our plans. He also uses those negative circumstances in our lives for our own good, if we are willing to respond to Him in humility, a teachable attitude and complete trust in the fact that He knows what is best for us. He is never caught off-guard because He knows the beginning and the ending before it happens. Furthermore, the God of the Bible thinks and behaves differently than we and is the God who is in control of all things.

Now what I've written is just a very small description of the God of the Bible. But it is my prayer that this short preview of the Biblical God will be enough for you to investigate Him further and develop a deep and personal confidence that He has your best interest at heart. He loves you and wants the best for you. And whether you are experiencing the good, bad or the ugly, He is ready to meet you where you are, walk you through the times of difficulty, and open a new and brighter future for you as you continue to place your confidence in Him.

12

The Story Transmitted

The Bible truly is a love story from God. It's His story about Himself, His love for mankind, and man's rebellion against a God who loves him and wants man to be with Him forever. But what we hold in our hands today as a Bible did not come in a beautiful leather-bound book when it was being written. In fact, you would never have recognized it in its early form.

Let me raise a question. How would we like to read a Bible that had no chapter divisions, no verses, and in the Old Testament, no vowels with the letters running together without any space in between the letters? In fact, we probably would not refer to it as one book. We would see it as 66 separate scrolls. We should be thankful that we are living in the Twenty-first Century.

Back in the 1960s, there was a famous coach who told his team that they needed to get back to the basics. His name was Vince Lombardi of the Green Bay Packers. Every year, when the new recruits came for the first session with their coach, Lombardi would say, *"Gentlemen, if we are going to be a winning team, we need to get back to the basics. So here it is."* He would then hold up a football and say, *"Gentlemen, this is a football"*. On one occasion, one of the seasoned players yelled, *"Hey coach, not so fast. Can you go a little slower?"*

As we continue to discover the love story in this amazing book, let's dig deeper into what I said in the Introduction. Let's get back to the basics. So here goes. Visualize me standing before you and holding up a Bible. Like Coach Lombardi, I'd say, *"This is what we call a Bible. It is divided into two sections: The Old Testament with 39 books and The New Testament with 27 books, totaling 66 books. The Old Testament focuses on mankind (Genesis 1-11), but especially on the nation of Israel (Genesis 12-Malachi), while the New Testament focus is on Jesus (Four Gospels), the Church (Acts & The Epistles – Letters written to individuals and churches) and the Future (Book of Revelation)"*. That's the Reader's Digest version of the Bible.

If we go to a bookstore to purchase a Bible today, we will open it and see that it is divided into 66 books, with chapter and verse divisions. It will have a Table of Contents to help find our way through those 66 books. And we may also find notes and references in the margins or at the bottom of the pages.

In chapter 13 we will discover how we got the English Bible, but here is a little preview of what it looked like before English was even a language. At the beginning, there were no chapter or verse divisions. A man named Stephen Langton, an Archbishop of Canterbury, added the chapter divisions around A.D. 1227. Then in A.D. 1448, Mordecai Nathan, a Jewish rabbi, divided the Old Testament into verses. Later in A.D. 1560 Robert Estienne, known as Stephanus, divided the New Testament into verses. We should appreciate the work of these three men who provided some great aids to help us make more sense out of what we are reading.

There is another group of men who made reading the Old Testament a lot easier for those who knew the Hebrew language. The Old Testament was written primarily in Hebrew. The Hebrew language is made up of 22 letters, compared to our English alphabet of 26 letters. However, all the letters are consonants. In other words, there were no vowels. Reading the Hebrew Bible would look something like this:

Genesis 1:1 in our Bible reads like this - *"In the beginning God created the heavens and earth"*. But if we read it in the Hebrew Bible it would look like this: **NTHBGNNNGGDCRT-DTHHVNSNDRTH.** However, since one reads Hebrew from right to left, it would look more like this – **HTRDNSNVHHTDTRCDG-GNNNGBHTN.**

This group of scribes were known as Masoretes (Tradition Keeper), most of whom lived in a city on the shores of the Sea of Galilee, called Tiberius from the 6th to 10th centuries A.D. If we were to go to Israel today, we would find it to be a thriving city. The Masoretes divided the words, added vowel points and put notes at the bottom of each page. This gave the reader a universal way to pronounce the words and made it a lot easier to read.

The Transmission Of God's Word

I shared this story earlier, but let's remind ourselves of it as we move from the mouth to the pen. God's Love Story began with His **REVELATION** to man. He made Himself known about 3,500 years ago to a man who was living in the desert. He was a shepherd and fugitive from Egypt because he had killed a man in Egypt and then fled into the desert to save his life. The man fled to Midian, located in present day Saudi Arabia. There he met his wife and began working for her father as a shepherd. In his case, this was a major downsizing. You see, prior to the murder, he was a Prince of Egypt, part of the royal family. He was well educated, knowing how to read and write. They called him Moses.

Let's review what I've said earlier about Moses. One day as he was attending his sheep, Moses noticed a burning bush. Though that was not unusual for bushes to spontaneously burst into flames in the desert, this bush was not consumed by the flame. As Moses approached the bush, a voice came from the bush saying, *"Moses, Moses!"* From that day on, Moses' life changed dramatically and set the stage for all mankind to possess the book we call the Bible.

God made Himself known to Moses and directed him to write the first five books of the Bible. God began the process by giving Moses Ten Commandments which God Himself wrote on tablets of stone. But Moses destroyed the tablets of stone due to anger against the Israelites for their unbelief. But the Lord had something that He wanted these people to know, so God carved the same Ten Commandments in stone a second time.

God's Word was first **REVEALED** to Moses and then **TRANSMITTED** through various channels. Though the first words of the Scripture were written on stone tablets, other materials were also available, including papyrus. In fact, the word *"Bible"* comes from the Greek word *"Biblos"*. Biblos was a port in Lebanon where Egyptians exported papyrus, a plant found in Egypt. Paper was made from the papyrus plant by separating it with a needlepoint into very thin strips. When the New Testament was first written, the writers used papyrus. However, when scribes copied from the original writings on papyri, they began to use parchment or leather.

Parchment comes from the Greek *"pergamene"* (Pergamum). Pergamum is a city in present day Turkey and was one of the seven churches to which the Book of Revelation was written (Revelation 2:12-17). The difference between leather and parchment is that chemical testing agents tan the leather, while parchment is stretched and dried on a frame. The word *"Vellum"* comes from the English *"veal"* (calf skin). It is a higher quality of leather.

But how did Moses hear about Abraham, Isaac and Jacob who lived before him? And where did he get his information on creation? Excellent questions! Before the written word, there was the spoken word. People and events were passed down within families from generation to generation. And since access to writing was scarce and most people were not literate, oral communication became the major means of communication.

Oral Communication To Written Communication

Because literacy is widespread in our generation and today we write, email, tweet and communicate by writing, it's difficult for us to comprehend oral communication as a legitimate and accurate means of conveying truth. Most of the time during a conversation, we are thinking more of what we are going to say next than we are listening to what the other person is telling us. next than we are listening to what the other person is telling us. However, in Biblical days, people carefully listened to the spoken word, many memorized what they heard and then passed on as it had been received.

Let me illustrate this fact with an event early in my life. Before God called me into ministry, I loved to hear Billy Graham on the radio (The Hour of Decision). At the age of eighteen, a friend invited me to go down to Ocean Grove, NJ and hear Graham in person in that beautiful old Ocean Grove Tabernacle. Listening to Billy preach in person was an eye opener. When I watched his body language and heard him say time and again, *"The Bible says*", I was much more aware of God's Presence in that meeting and I could capture more of what Graham was attempting to communicate.

The problem with written communication is that the reader misses the nuances of the writer. How often have you written an email to someone who totally misunderstood what you were attempting to say? They could only read your words, but missed your intent. They didn't see your eyes nor could they read your body language. They may have thought that you were angry, when you had no anger toward them at all. On the other hand, oral communication can often be more effective because you know when a person is serious, humorous, bored, or angry. You read body language as well as listen to the words. In Biblical days, oral communication was accurately passed on from generation to generation.

But once the speaker is no longer with us, we're glad that he wrote something that we can hold on to. For instance, my mother went to be with the Lord when I was only 21 years old. I no longer can see her laugh, hear her voice or feel her arms around me. But I do treasure the letters that she left behind. Written communication becomes extremely valuable when the authors of that communication are no longer with us. And as the persecutions of the early Church set in, men began to put their words into written communication. In addition, the Bible itself affirms that it was God Himself who superintended the communication of truth from generation to generation (2 Peter 1:21).

Written By Man, But Authored By God

The **Apostle Peter** was convinced that this amazing love story originated from God – "*Above all, you must understand that no* *prophecy of Scripture came about by the prophet's own interpretation. For prophecy never had its origin in the will of man, but men spoke from God as they were carried along by the Holy Spirit"* (2Peter 1:20-21). He further stated that the Apostle Paul's writing was from God, for he called it "Scripture", meaning the written Word of God. Peter stated, *"His (Paul's) letters contain some things that are hard to understand, which ignorant and unstable people distort, as they do the other Scriptures, to their own destruction"* (2Peter 3:16).

The **Apostle Paul** held the same conviction, for he wrote the following words: *"What advantage, then, is there in being a Jew, or what value is there in circumcision? Much in every way! First, they have been entrusted with the very words of God"* (Romans 3:1-2). He further wrote, *"All Scripture is God-breathed and is useful for teaching, rebuking, correcting and training in righteousness, so that the man of God may be thoroughly equipped for every good work"* (2Timothy 3:16-17).

Would Jesus agree with these Apostles? **Jesus** Himself accepted the Old Testament as God's Word, including the oral and written communication of people and events. When He addressed the religious leaders of His day, the Lord rebuked them, saying, *"Thus you nullify the word of God by your tradition that you have handed down. And you do many things like that"* (Mark 7:13). He also claimed that the Psalms of the Old Testament spoke about Him. He told His disciples, *"This is what I told you while I was still with you: Everything must be fulfilled that is written about me in the Law of Moses, the Prophets and the Psalms"* (Luke 24:44). The Jewish Bible was divided into the Law and the Prophets (Luke 24:27), but the Psalms especially revealed the coming Messiah. He claimed that we can find information about Him throughout the entire Old Testament, including what was handed down orally and what was written. The Jews were looking for their Messiah because

Moses spoke about Him in the first five books of the Bible. In addition, David spoke about Him in the Psalms and the Prophets spoke about Him in their prophesies.

Either Peter, Paul and Jesus were telling the truth or they would have to be considered as liars, deceivers, or something worse. In other words, the Bible itself claims to be the written revelation of God to man.

We've seen how God guided the communication of His will and words through oral communication to writing. But how did we get the Bible in the English language? What process did God use to get the Bible into our hands so we could understand His heart and plan for us? Read on and meet a man by the name of John Wycliffe.

13

The Story Translated

Not only is the Love Story from God expanded, explained, and completed in the last Book of the Bible, but it is also expressed in many translations of Scripture. We learned in the last chapter that the Bible that you and I hold in our hands did not always look that way. In fact, if we possessed what was written, when it was written, we would not even be able to read it because the Bible was first written in three different languages, Hebrew, Greek and Aramaic. Moreover, any copies of the Scriptures were quite rare, so you most likely would never have owned a copy. And if you could have owned copies of the entire Bible, those copies would not be in a book form. Instead you would have to cart around with you sixty-six scrolls, some of which were very heavy and large, such as the Isaiah scroll.

So how did men express this Love Story from Hebrew, Aramaic, Greek, and Latin to English? Another question needed answered is how did the first English translation birth so many other translations? It is a love story from God, but while one English translation of that story seems archaic to some, another translation may seem too flippant to others. What was the process that

God used to guarantee that what we have in our hands today is an accurate copy of what God wanted us to possess?

These are all good questions, so walk with me mentally as we journey back through history and learn of this unique process that brought us a trustworthy Book that expresses God's love for us, and holds the secrets of a meaningful life on earth and the promise of eternal life when our souls exit our bodies.

The first indication that God wanted man to have a **"written"** record of His character and works was when He called Moses up to the top of Mt. Sinai and said, *"Come up to me on the mountain and stay here, and I will give you the tablets of stone, with the law and commands I have written for their instruction"* (Exodus 24:12). However, when Moses discovered that the people had already rebelled against God, he threw down the stone tablets in a rage of anger, shattering the very words of God.

That could have been the end of God's communication to man, but He is a loving, merciful and forgiving God, so He called Moses back to the top of the mountain again. *"The Lord said to Moses, 'Chisel out two stone tablets like the first ones, and I will write on them the words that were on the first tablets, which you broke'"* (Exodus 34:1). Today we should be thrilled that we've moved from stone tablets to paper and electronic software. Just think of the progress we've made.

The Lord spoke many more words to Moses, resulting in the first five Books of the Bible, also known as the Torah. But the Lord had a lot more to say to His people Israel, and so He continued to speak through many others over the years including poets, prophets, kings, fishermen, shepherds, tax collectors, political zealots, doctors, and even men sitting in prison. The writing moved from stone to papyri and finally to parchment (animal skin). And eventually scrolls gave way to books (codices). But what about the language issues? How did we get our English bibles that we use today? To answer this question, we'll look back to the ancient texts of Hebrew, Greek and Aramaic.

The Old Testament was primarily written in the Hebrew language, with some sections including some Aramaic, which is similar with Hebrew. But when Alexander the Great expanded his empire, Greek became the language of most countries, even in Egypt. Because of this language change, the Jews living in Alexandria, Egypt were recognizing that the generation after them would probably speak Greek as their mother tongue. The Jews of Alexandria wanted to be able to read the Bible in their native tongue (Greek). Because of this built-up desire, the Egyptian ruler, Ptolemy II Philadelphus (285-247 B.C.) commissioned and paid for a Greek translation of the Hebrew Bible. They called it The Septuagint Translation and it became the Bible of Jesus and the Apostles. On the other hand, the New Testament was written in Greek so that the entire world would be able to read its pages. And it also contained a few Aramaic phrases.

But the translations did not stop with Greek. Other nations wanted this love story from God translated into their language, so more and more translations appeared. The Coptic Translation (Egypt), and the Syriac Translation (Syria) were two of the earliest new translations.

THE LATIN VULGATE (400 A.D.) - By 382 A.D. Latin had become the official language in the West, and so the demand for a Latin translation soon became evident to all. Various attempts for a Latin translation were made, but they were not very good. To address this problem, in 382 A.D. Damasus, Bishop of Rome commissioned a priest by the name of Jerome to provide an accurate translation in the Latin tongue. That translation became known as the Vulgate and lasted for 1,000 years. Jerome was quite a scholar and knew the original languages of Hebrew and Greek. He even moved to Bethlehem and finished his translation in a cave.

Jerome provided the world with a good translation, but as time passed, the Latin language began to fade. That meant that the common man's knowledge of Scripture was completely dependent upon what the priests said. There was no means by which anyone could evaluate what was being spoken from the pulpit

THE WYCLIFFE BIBLE (1380 A.D.) - But a thousand years later, everything changed. A priest, who was also an Oxford scholar named John Wycliffe, entered the scene. He had developed a heart for the common man and desperately wanted to put a Bible in the hands of the commoner so that everyone could experience the love story from His Creator. As time passed, Wycliffe recognized that the church was becoming more and more corrupt with wealth and power. Therefore, he began to write tracts and books that exposed this corruption. While the church determined that it was the final authority in spiritual matters, Wycliffe became more and more convinced that the Bible alone was the sole authority and eventually became known as "The Morning Star of the Reformation".

At that time the French had the Bible in their language, but not the English. Therefore, Wycliffe began to translate portions of the Scriptures into English. He translated the New Testament from Latin, but a man named Nicholas de Hereford translated most of the Old Testament. Eventually, Wycliffe was excommunicated and left England. Wycliffe completed what was remaining in the Old Testament translation by his friend Nicholas.

Since the printing press had not yet been developed, Wycliffe's Bibles were *"handwritten"* primarily by the Lollards, poor Oxford scholars, who traveled the country preaching and teaching God's Word. They helped Wycliffe in his translation, writing each copy by hand. However, many of them lost their lives by being burned at the stake or hanged. Wycliffe was fired from his post at Oxford in 1382 and the Pope issued numerous edicts for his arrest.

John Wycliffe continued to write and preach about the corruption in the church until he suffered a stroke and died on December 31, 1384. And though he died a natural death, forty years later the religious authorities dug up his bones and burned them, accusing Wycliffe of heresy for translating the Bible into the language of the common man.

By the year 1408 it became illegal to translate or even read the Bible in English without the permission of the Bishop. Besides this law, those in authority saw little need for an English translation. Per Dr. Dan Wallace, *"Noblemen wrote in French – the language of the elite –and official church documents were in Latin. English was for peasants"*.[1] And though there are few remaining copies of the handwritten Wycliffe Bible, his memory and work continue through such organizations as the Wycliffe Bible Translators.

This great organization was started back in 1917 – *"In 1917 a missionary named William Cameron Townsend went to*

---

1. Dan Wallace, The Biblical Studies Foundation (www.bible.org), p.2003.

Guatemala to sell Spanish Bibles. But he was shocked when many people couldn't understand the books. They spoke Cakchiquel, a language without a Bible. Cam believed everyone should understand the Bible, so he started a linguistics school (the Summer Institute of Linguistics, known today as SIL) that trained people to do Bible translation. The work continued to grow, and in 1942 Cam officially founded Wycliffe Bible Translators.

Over the following decades, Wycliffe celebrated many mile-stones — from the first translation completed in 1951, all the way to the 500th translation completed in 2000. Around the same time, Wycliffe adopted a new challenge — a goal of starting a Bible translation project in every language still needing one by 2025."[1]

I had the privilege of meeting Cameron years ago when we were both speaking at a Bible Conference facility in Boca Raton, FL. He was then in his eighties and as full of life as a man in his sixties. The Lord has used Cam to bring about beautiful changes in the lives of people that the rest of the world never noticed.

About 150 years after John Wycliffe passed off the scene, God raised up a printer and a translator. The printer's name was Johannes Gutenberg who invented the printing press in 1439-40. Then in 1452, he printed the first Bible to come off a printing press. It was a Latin translation of the Bible, but the fact that a Bible could be printed, gave birth to a widespread passion for the Bible in other languages. Besides being handwritten, the Wycliffe Bible was written in Old English. By the time Gutenberg invented the printing press and another translator came on the scene, the English language was still developing.

---

1. xxxxxxxx

THE TYNDALE BIBLE (1525 A.D.) – About 150 years after Wycliffe, a translator named William Tyndale shared his passion in a heated discussion with a fellow cleric when he said, *"If God spare my life, ere many years I will cause a boy that driveth the plough, shall know more of the Scripture than thou dost!"* He also wanted to get this love story from God into the hands of the common man, so that they would be able to experience His love and discern truth from error.

William Tyndale studied at both Oxford and Cambridge. He spoke seven languages. Furthermore, he was proficient in both Hebrew and Greek. Therefore, he translated from the original languages rather than the Latin Vulgate, as Wycliffe had done. His New Testament translation was the first English New Testament from the Greek language. Tyndale attempted on numerous occasions to get support from church authorities to translate the Bible into English, but instead of support, he experienced indifference and even threats.

Because it was almost impossible to do any translating in England, due to the1408 edit against translating the Bible into English, Tyndale went to Germany under an assumed name. There he met with Martin Luther, who was in the process of translating the Bible into German. Though Tyndale wanted to return to England, he knew that he would be taking his life into his own hands. It has been estimated that there were over seventy-two thousand executions under Henry VIII's reign.

Therefore, Tyndale began his translation work in Germany (1525-35) and smuggled his Bibles into England. He evaded authorities for nine years. However, Henry Phillips, a friend of Tyndale, deceived him and Tyndale was arrested. The authorities put Tyndale into a cold, damp dungeon for a time and eventually choked him to death and then burned him at the stake. Many of the translations following Tyndale were based upon his translation, including the King James Version. His friend Miles Coverdale picked up the mantle and finished Tyndale's translation, which became known as the Coverdale Bible.

Just as Wycliffe's legacy continues in the form of the Wycliffe Bible Translators, so does Tyndale's legacy live on through another great organization, thanks to a man who became a friend over the years. I am referring to Dr. Kenneth Taylor, the translator of the Living Bible that was later retranslated and is now known as The New Living Translation. Ken was also the founder of Tyndale House Publishers, named after William Tyndale. And he was also the man who encouraged me back in 1973 to write a book that eventually became a best seller entitled *"Discover Your Spiritual Gift And Use It"*.

Literally millions of lives have been touched by both the Living Bible and the New Living Translation. One day we were having lunch together and Ken shared with me how he came up with the idea of translating the Living Bible. He had quite a large family of 10 children. Each evening he wanted to have family devotions and would read from the only English Bible available at that time, The King James Bible. His children became very fidgety as they endured Ken's attempt to keep their attention as he read in Old English. He soon came to realize that he was facing a major problem.

During this time, Ken was working at Moody Press in Chicago while living in Wheaton, IL. He took the train into the big city each morning and used that time to translate. It took him a half hour each way, so Ken worked each day on his translation for a solid hour without interruption. Eventually he completed the Epistles and called them the Living Letters.

When Billy Graham saw a copy of the Living Letters, He asked permission to reprint them and give them away as gifts on the telecasts of his crusades. Half a million copies were given away at the crusades. Ken then moved on to translate the rest of the New Testament which was completed in 1967. By 1971 Ken finished the entire Bible and called it The Living Bible. It sold over 40,000 million copies.

Ken was motivated by the story of William Tyndale and was just as committed to get the Bible into the hands of the everyday man on the street. Because of his efforts thousands of men and women have a personal relationship the Lord Jesus Christ and are growing in His wisdom and knowledge through reading The New Living Translation.

William Tyndale never finished the Old Testament before he was choked to death and then burned at the stake, but his New Testament was completed and was translated from the Erasmus Greek text, 3rd edition. In the next few pages you will learn more about that Greek text and why it is significant.

THE COVERDALE BIBLE (1535 A.D.) - The next English translation to share God's love story was produced in 1535 by Miles Coverdale, Tyndale's assistant. His translation was the first complete Bible that was printed in English. Coverdale's Bible did not contain either contentious prefaces or notes that could be found in Tyndale's Bible. Furthermore, it contained a dedication to the king. Thus, it was more acceptable than Tyndale's Bible.

THE MATTHEW'S BIBLE (1537 A.D.) - Two years after Coverdale completed his translation, the Matthew-Tyndale Bible was made available to the public. This translation was a combination of both the Tyndale and Coverdale Bibles and translated by John Rogers, who used the pen name of Thomas Matthew. It was the first Bible published with the king's permission and even gives a tribute to William Tyndale on the last page of the

Old Testament. In addition, The Bible was a combination of Coverdale's Old Testament and Tyndale's New Testament. Rogers added 2,000 notes to his translation. However, in 1555 Rogers became the first martyr under Mary Tudor, who was the Catholic monarch.

THE GREAT BIBLE (1539 A.D.) - Following Matthew's Bible, the advisor to King Henry the VIII asked Coverdale to revise Matthew's Bible. In 1538 the King had ordered that an English Bible be placed in every church, which encouraged Coverdale to complete the task quickly. In 1539 Coverdale released **The Great Bible**. This Bible was very similar with the Matthew's Bible, but without the 2,000 notes attached. It was known as the Great Bible due to its size and weight. Sometimes it was referred to as the *"Chained Bible"* because it was chained to the pillars of the church for fear of someone removing it from the church.

This Bible was the first commissioned English Bible, planned by Thomas Cromwell and approved by Archbishop Crammer. Though many laymen greatly appreciated hearing this Bible read from the pulpits each week, many of the Bishops were Roman Catholic and were offended for two reasons: First, this Bible separated the Apocrypha (disputed books included in the Catholic and Greek Orthodox Bibles) from the rest of the Old Testament and placed it in the Appendix. Second, it wasn't translated from the Latin Vulgate.

THE GENEVA BIBLE (1560 A.D.) - In 1553 Mary Tudor came to power and turned England back into a Catholic nation. She not only burned Bibles but also burned Protestants at the stake. She became known as "Bloody Mary". Many scholars fled to Geneva, Switzerland and wanted a Bible of their own. This was the home of John Calvin, the great reformer of the Reformation. His brother-in-law William Whittingham, along with other scholars, translated the Bible which became known as the Geneva Bible, a complete revision of the Great Bible. This Bible contained many notes that were very "Calvinistic" in theology. By this I mean that the notes were theological notes that favored John Calvin's theological positions, focusing on the glory of the Lord.

It was also the first Bible to include divisions for the verses thanks to the work of Stephanus' fourth edition of the Greek New Testament of 1551. It became the Bible of the Pilgrims when they came to America and it had great influence on the King James Bible. It was also the Bible that Shakespeare read. The Geneva Bible was very popular for fifty years. However, though the lower classes loved this translation, many of the clergy did not because of the notes throughout the Bible.

THE BISHOPS BIBLE (1568 A.D.) - The Bishops wanted a translation of their own. This led to the "Bishop's Bible" (1568), translated by eight Bishops of the Church of England and under the reign of Queen Elizabeth in 1568. However, she never fully recognized it. Furthermore, this Bible was not very good for reading in public. Its quality was inconsistent and when people heard it read, they thought it was stiff and much too formal.

THE DOUAY-RHEIMS BIBLE (1610 A.D.) (sometimes called the **RHEIMS-DOUAI BIBLE** - 1610) – Not to be outdone by the Protestants, the Catholics wanted their own translation. The result was a Bible translated with the Apocrypha in the Old Testament and Catholic notes and explanations. It was a rather poor translation and did not use either the Hebrew or Greek manuscripts, but relied solely upon the Latin translation. And from a chronological standpoint, this brings us to a translation on which I was reared and one that has lasted more than 500 years to this very day. I'm referring to the King James Bible.

You might think that with all these translations available in English, there was no more need to translate another version of Scripture. But not all translations are the result of prayerful decisions by committed believers. When religion and the government were intertwined, politics often ruled in the decisions of translations. Such was the case for the King James Translation of Scripture.

THE KING JAMES BIBLE (1611) – Many people today are under the impression that King James translated it. There are others who believe that it is the only Bible one should read. And it is probably one of the most controversial translations today because of the manuscripts from which it was translated, especially the New Testament. But before we look at the actual process of translating the KJV, allow me to share a little side bar.

When King James became James I of England he had already ruled over Scotland for thirty-seven years with the title James VI. In 1604 nearly one thousand Puritan leaders had signed grievances against the Church of England. Though King James treated the Puritans badly, John Reynolds, Puritan President of Corpus Christi College, Oxford, raised the issue of having an *"authorized"* Bible for everyone in the church. James favored the idea because of the divisions within the church parties and he wanted to replace the Geneva and Bishops' Bibles.

He assembled fifty-four translators and out of them, forty-seven men worked on the revision of the Bishops' Bible which would become the KJV. James assigned six panels of scholars to work on the new translation. Three of them focused on the Old Testament, two on the New Testament, and one panel worked on the Apocrypha. The difficulty they faced was the fact that only six Greek manuscripts were available for their use in translating the New Testament.

Furthermore, those half-dozen manuscripts did not extend back any further than the twelfth to the fifteenth centuries. Why is that important? Because the closer you can get to the original writings of the New Testament writers (Paul, Matthew, Mark, Luke, John, Peter, etc.), the purer the text will be. For instance, the Book of Revelation was written at the close of the first century (95-100 A.D.). Therefore, if you could find Greek manuscripts that dated back to the second, third or fourth centuries, they would be closer to the original writings than if you found manuscripts that were a thousand years further away from the original writings.

The Greek manuscripts used by the King James translators came from the 3rd edition of Erasmus' Greek text. Erasmus was a famous Renaissance scholar (1496-1536). He published the first edition of a Greek New Testament by using six Greek manuscripts dating to the twelfth century and later. It was deficient in that it did not have access to some other older manuscripts and Greek papyri because they had not yet surfaced. Later, others built upon his Greek text and translated their own. Eventually these texts became known as the "Textus Receptus" or "Received Text". And for the King James New Testament, the translators used this text from which to translate it into English.

It took six committees, two bishops, one archbishop, and twelve reviewers to complete the translation. Though this new translation was quite eloquent and a *"word-for-word"* translation, many problems emerged from the early copies. For instance, it became known as the *"wicked Bible"* because of one word that erroneously was omitted from one of the Ten Commandments. The seventh commandment of this early KJV read, "Thou *shalt commit adultery"*.

The more the translators worked on this new translation, it looked like a mere revision of the Tyndale Bible and the Bishops'

Bible. In fact, it could be regarded as the fifth revision of the Tyndale Bible because 90% of the New Testament is from the Tyndale Bible. Where it differed from Tyndale was that it replaced accuracy for eloquence. It also placed the Apocrypha at the end of the Old Testament.

Another feature of this new translation was the number of notes that it included – nearly 8,500 marginal notes, many of which explained that the translators were undecided concerning the meaning of the original text.

In his lectures to the students at Lancaster Bible College in Lancaster, PA, Dr. Dan Wallace made the following observations about the King James Bible. They included: *(1) The translators do not equate their work with the inspired word of God; they explicitly deny the perfection of the KJB. (2) They freely admit that even the worst translation of Scripture is still to be regarded as the Word of God. (3) They make a qualitative distinction between the text written in one language and the translation of it into another. Regarding Scripture, they admit that only the original text in Greek and Hebrew was inspired (4) They implicitly approve all later revisions of their own work, because the very nature of Bible translation involves 'a history of repeated revision and correction.'"*.[1]

The King James Translation at first experienced scathing reviews due to its inaccuracies. In fact, in the first three years this new translation went through fourteen minor editions because of mistakes in the process of translating and printing. Furthermore, they have made nearly 100,000 changes to the 1611 version. And what you and I might have at home as our KJV, is not the 1611 version. Instead, the King James Bibles of today come from the 1769 edition of the KJV.

---

1. Dan Wallace. The Biblical Studies Foundation (www.bible.org)

And yet, the King James Version of the Bible is not only the most popular Bible in history, it has also been the most influential book in the history of the English language.[1] In his book entitled *"The Story of The Bible"*, Larry Stone states, *"The influence of the King James Version on English civilization has been profound. It has helped form our language; it has given context to our literature; it has inspired our music; and for centuries it was the one book a family would own and read before all others"*.[2]

The Attempted Improvements Of The KJB

This version maintained its popularity for over 450 years. But back in 1870 a British church commissioned an updated version of the KJB due to many new manuscripts that were not available in 1611. The British version was completed in 1885 and they called it The **English Revised Version.**

Then in 1901 an American Version was completed and was known as the **American Standard Version (ASV)**. And in 1952 the **Revised Standard Version (RSV)** was produced. However, since it was approved by the National Council of Churches that included most of the mainline denominations and slanted to a more liberal theological viewpoint, it was condemned by many Evangelicals.

The primary reason for this was the way the translators translated the Hebrew word *"alma"* in Isaiah 7:14. The word

---

1. Arnold, Clinton E. 2008. *How We Got The Bible*. Grand Rapids, MI: Zondervan. 64
2. Larry Stone. 2001. *The Story of The Bible*. Nashville, TN: Thomas Nelson. 77

could be translated either *"young woman"* or *"virgin"*. This was very important because Matthew interprets that word as *"virgin"* when he writes, *"All this took place to fulfill what the Lord had said through the prophet: 'The virgin will be with child and will give birth to a son, and they will call him Immanuel' – which means, 'God with us'"* (Matthew 1:22-23). However, the translators of the RSV decided to translate the word as *"young woman"* – *"Therefore the Lord himself will give you a sign. Behold, a **young woman** shall conceive and bear a son, and shall call his name Immanuel"*.

Almost twenty years later (1971) the Lockman Foundation commissioned its own revision of the ASV, but decided on a more word-for-word translation of the Bible. This resulted in the **New American Standard Bible (NASB).** However, the RSV, ASV and the NASB were all revisions of the King James Bible. The language was still different from the way many of us speak today.

A NEW KIND OF TRANSLATION - While the NASB was an excellent translation of the Bible, it was not that great for a *"pulpit Bible"*, one that I read and from which I preached. It was in the same year when the NASB was introduced to the public that Dr. Kenneth Taylor, about whom we referred to earlier, entered the scene with his vision for a new translation of the Bible. He envisioned a translation that younger children could understand. This resulted in **The Living Bible (1971),** which was more of a paraphrase than a translation.

THE NIV – A TOTALLY NEW REVISION - Since the ASV, RSV and NASB were all revisions of the King James Bible, some men saw the need for a translation that went back to the original languages and used the many Greek manuscripts that were available for the New Testament and the Dead Sea Scrolls for the Old Testament. A completely original version, translated by more than 100 scholars began the new translation. The preface of the NIV reads, *"The New International Version is a completely new translation of the Holy Bible made by over a hundred scholars working directly from the best available Hebrew, Aramaic and Greek texts."*[1] Their stated goals were *"that it would be an accurate translation and one that would have clarity and literary quality and so prove suitable for public and private reading, teaching, preaching, memorizing and liturgical use"*[2]

Then in the 1980s more translations emerged on the scene such as the New King James Version (NKJV) in 1982, the New Revised Standard Version (gender neutral) of 1989, the Contemporary English Version of 1991, God's Word of 1995, the New Living Translation of 1996, the Holman Christian Standard Bible (H.C.S.B.) of 2000, the English Standard Version of 2001 (ESV), Today's New International Version of 2001 (T.N.I.V.), The Message of 2002, and the New English Translation (NET) of 2005 which is free online, but also available in hard cover.

There are numerous reasons why so many modern translations have hit the market in recent years, but here are two major motivating factors: (1) the Dead Sea Scroll discovery for the comparison of the Old Testament accuracy and (2) the availability of over 5800 Greek manuscripts for comparison of the New Testament's accuracy.

By this time, you may be wondering, *"How am I to choose a translation?"* Good question because it all does seem confusing. Let me answer that question by first letting you know that there are three major ways that Bibles are translated: (1) A word-for-word translation; (2) A thought-for-thought translation; and (3) A

1. *The New International Version.* 1996. Nashville, TN: Broadman & Holman Publishers. Preface

2. Ibid

paraphrase. So here are some guidelines for choosing what translation you could consider for reading and studying.

1. For Personal Study, choose more of a word-for-word translation such as the NASB or the ESV.
2. For public reading, choose more of a thought-for-thought translation such as the NIV or NLT.
3. For personal reading so you capture the sense of the writer, choose more of a paraphrase such as The Living Bible or The Message. However, never develop your theology based on a paraphrase.
4. For deeper study of God's Word, choose any one of the *"Study Bibles"* such as the Net Bible, the Ryrie Study Bible, the Zondervan Study Bible, and other such Bibles that have a lot of cross references and notes.

CHAPTER

14

Can We Trust This Story?

As you read this chapter, you'll notice that it is a little different from previous chapters because it is more of a defense for the trustworthiness of the Bible. It will focus more on evidence than on life stories.

Now that you've gained an overview of the Bible, another question arises – can I trust it? Let's think about that. It's an excellent question. After all, we're dealing with an ancient Book, written over a 1500-year time-frame in three languages on three continents by forty writers. None of us have ever met any of these men, and there are no living eye-witnesses that could verify the truthfulness of any statement in the Bible. Therefore, the question is legitimate.

We can add to this that the Old Testament was not accepted as God's Word by any religious group until around 400 B.C. To make matters worse, we have none of the original writings, nor do we have that many copies of copies of copies that date back to the first and second centuries. So how can we say that the Bible is truly the Word of God? Well, let's look at some important evidence. We'll begin with the manuscripts.

Manuscripts – Examine the Scrolls
The Reliability of the Old Testament

What is a manuscript? It is basically anything written by hand, but we will refer to those documents of the Bible that were written in the original tongue, which in the Old Testament was primarily Hebrew and in the New Testament was primarily Greek.

There are not too many Hebrew manuscripts available for several reasons. First, we must recognize that the nation of Israel was removed from their land, first by the Assyrians in 722 B.C. and then by the Babylonians in 586 B.C. Not only were the people removed from the land, but their Temple was destroyed, along with the city of Jerusalem and any Hebrew manuscripts that existed. Secondly, when a Hebrew manuscript became old and worn, the religious leaders buried those manuscripts and replaced them with new copies.

However, what we have in our Old Testament today is 100% dependable. Why do I say that? Because those scrolls were accepted by Israel for hundreds of years before Christ came to earth. Furthermore, it was the Bible of Jesus and the Apostles, though they primarily quoted from the Septuagint translation (the Hebrew Bible translated into Greek). And it was the Bible of the early Church.

Another reason we can depend on our Old Testament was the care taken by the Hebrew scribes when they copied from one manuscript to another. Consider the rules imposed upon the scribes as they copied from one manuscript to another.

1. No individual **letter** could be written down without having looked back at the copy in front of them.

2. The scribe could not write **God's name** with a newly dipped pen (lest it blotch). Even if the king should address him while writing God's name, he should take no notice of him.
3. The scribe counted the **paragraphs, words,** and **letters** so he could know by counting, if he had done it perfectly.
4. He knew the **middle** letter of each book so he could count back and see if he had missed anything.

Geisler and Nix write, *"Of the 166 words in Isaiah 53, there are only 17 letters in question. . . Thus, in one chapter of 166 words, there is only **one word** (three letters) in question after a thousand years of transmission - and this word does not significantly change the meaning of the passage."*[1]

A final reason emerges from comparing later manuscripts with earlier manuscripts. For instance, up to 1948, the oldest Hebrew manuscript that existed with the Aleppo Codex, dated to 920 A.D. Let me explain some terminology. A codex is basically a book form of a series of manuscripts. When the original writings were produced, they were written primarily on papyri and parchment. It was easy to write on, but perishable over time. Eventually, copies of manuscripts were written on parchment, or animal skin. But as the scrolls were collected and several Books were combined, the scroll became extremely heavy and long. Therefore, it became essential to cut the scrolls into similar size sheets of parchment and sew them together. This became a codex.

Aleppo is a city in Syria and much in the news even today because it had become a haven for ISIS. The Codex was written in

---

1. Geisler, Norman and Nix, William. 1974. A General Introduction To The Bible. Chicago, IL: Moody Press. 263.

920 A.D. around the city of Tiberius, on the Sea of Galilee in Israel. For about five centuries, it was kept in the synagogue in Aleppo, Syria. In 1948 rioters set the synagogue on fire. Today we possess two-thirds of the codex and no one knows whether the rest was destroyed by the fire or hidden somewhere.

Another ancient codex can be found in Leningrad, Russia and is called the Leningrad Codex, dating to 1010 A.D. This was the earliest complete Hebrew manuscript in existence. This means that to determine how accurate our Old Testament was, we had to compare it with a manuscript that was 1100 years closer to the original writings that what we possess today. But what if we could go back another 1,000 years or more. That would get us very close to when the last Book of the Old Testament (Malachi) was written in 450 B.C. What if we could get within two hundred years of that last Book?

Enter the Dead Sea Scrolls. In 1947 a young shepherd was down in the Dead Sea area of Israel looking for his goats. The area was filled with caves. As he spotted one of the caves, he decided to throw a stone into one of the caves and he heard a "clink". That was unusual. He should not have heard anything. But he couldn't get the *"clink"* out of his mind, so he decided to move up to the cave. As he entered it, he noticed some good-size jars. When he reached into the jars, he found a lot of manuscripts, but had no idea what

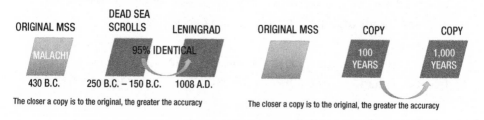

Figure 26 - Chart by Dr. Rick Yohn

they were or their value. Soon word got out about this significant discovery, and manuscript scholars began to realize what was in those caves and so the hunt began.

What did they find in those eleven caves near the Dead Sea? *"Among the twenty-eight nearly complete scrolls and 100,000 fragments of another 875 manuscripts, multiple portions of every book of the Hebrew Bible (except Esther) were present. These Hebrew, Aramaic, and Greek manuscripts became the oldest representatives of the Old Testament text available, pushing back the date of our earliest biblical manuscripts by 1,000 years."*[1] This is where the famous Isaiah Scroll was found intact. And if you were to compare the Book of Isaiah in your Bible to that Scroll, you would discover a 99% accuracy. Imagine, a Bible in the 21st Century is identical to a scroll that is approximately 2300 years closer to the original writing. How is that for transmitting a very accurate text?

Several years ago, I had the privilege of visiting the Shrine of The Book to see a portion of the Isaiah Scroll, found in that cave by the Dead Sea. As I gazed upon it, I began to wish that I had paid more attention to my Hebrew professors in seminary. I would love to have compared it to my Hebrew Bible, but I confess, I would have failed that test. However, my good friend, Amir Tsarfati, a major in the Israeli Defense Force and my tour guide on several tours to Israel, did exactly that. He took his Hebrew Bible to the Shrine of the Book and read from the Isaiah scroll and then checked it with his Bible. The result? Total accuracy between the two.

---

1. Clinton E. Arnold, *How We Got The Bible: A Visual Journey* (Grand Rapids, MI: Zondervan, 2008) p.16.

The Reliability Of The New Testament

But what about the New Testament? How do those manuscripts compare to what we have in our possession today? While the Hebrew manuscripts are few and far between, we have what Dr. Dan Wallace of Dallas Theological Seminary calls *"an embarrassment of riches"*. Though there are a handful of Hebrew manuscripts, we possess almost 6,000 Greek manuscripts that we can compare with one another for accuracy. Most of the manuscripts date back to the third and fourth century A.D., with some dating back to the second century. As scholars compare manuscript with manuscript, they discovered that 99% of the differences in the texts are common spelling differences or having a definite article in one manuscript, but missing in another. And in 100% of the differences, there is no issue in any doctrine of the faith.

- Many manuscripts of antiquity are separated by hundreds of years between the original text and the earliest copies.
- But for the New Testament, from the original to the earliest copies
  a) 114 fragments are **50** years separated from the original manuscript
  b) What does all this 200 books are **100** years separated from the original manuscript
  c) What does all this 325 complete New Testament copies are only **225** years from the original text

When compared with other ancient manuscripts, it is obvious that the New Testament manuscripts that we have for comparison are much earlier than other ancient manuscripts. Furthermore, we have far more copies which we can use for comparison. Josh McDowell quotes Ravi Zacharias saying, *"In real terms, the New Testament is easily the best attested ancient writing in terms of the sheer number of documents, the time span between the events and the document, and the variety of documents available to sustain or contradict it. There is nothing in ancient manuscript evidence to match such textual availability and integrity."*[1]

What does that tell us? It guarantees that what you hold in your hand as your Bible is what the original writers wrote thousands of years ago. God's love story to you is true. That's evidence of the Apostle Paul's words when he wrote, *"All Scripture is **God-breathed** and is useful for teaching, rebuking, correcting and training in righteousness, so that the man of God may be thoroughly equipped for every good work"* (2 Timothy 3:16-17).

Archaeology – Consider The Trowel And The Sifting Screen

Why do I say that we should consider the trowel and the sifting screen? If you've ever seen photos or videos of an archaeologist uncovering relics from the past, he/she usually uses a trowel and a sifting screen, among other instruments. He must be very careful not to destroy any of the artifacts he is uncovering.

What do we mean when we speak about archaeology? Archaeology is the *"scientific excavation and study of ancient human material remains"*.[2] I've had the privilege of subscribing to and reading BAR Magazine (Bible Archaeological Review) since the 1970s. I first became fascinated by this scientific study in the 1980s when my secretary's father died. He was a pastor who collected

---

1. Ibid, 35.

2. Introduction To Archaeology: Glossary. Archaeological Institute of America. archaeological.org

BAR Magazine since its inception. His wife gave me his collection and I have been interested in archaeology ever since.

I acknowledge that archaeology does not *"prove"* the Bible, but it does provide evidence of the Bible's accuracy. To date, no archaeological finding has disproved anything from Scripture, but rather it affirms the teaching of Scripture, including real locations, real people, and real historical events recorded in the Bible.

For years, skeptics proclaimed that there never was a *"House of David"* or a Davidic Kingdom. And then a funny thing happened during an excavation up in the city of Dan. It was there in 1994, that they found a *"stele"* or large stone that had an inscription reading, *"the house of David"*. It is known as the *"Tel-Dan Stele"*. The word *"Tel"* comes from an Arabic term meaning *"mound,"* or *"mount."* Cities in ancient times were built, destroyed, rebuilt on the same site and then destroyed again and rebuilt. This resulted in a *"mound"* of several layers of civilization. The word *"stele"* is an upright slab of wood or stone that commemorated a specific event. Often a stele was set up as a monument.

Another disclaimer by many skeptics was the existence of anyone by the title, "Pontius Pilate", the Roman Procurator, who set the robber Barabbas free and sent Jesus to the cross. But in 1961, that claim was put to rest permanently when archaeologists found a stone in Caesarea, Israel with the following inscription – *"Pontius Pilate, Prefect of Judaea, made and dedicated the Tiberieum to the Divine Augustus"*. Yes, there was Pontius Pilate who sentenced Jesus of Nazareth to death.

Skeptics also questioned the existence of Caiaphas, the High Priest, to whom Jesus was taken for interrogation the night He was betrayed. But in December of 1990, an ossuary (burial box) was found with the following inscription, *"Joseph son of (or, of the family of) Caiaphas"*. Did this result in an apology from the skeptics? Did they then say, we were wrong? I'll let you decide those questions.

These are just three of many archaeological discoveries that provide evidence to support the validity of Scripture. It is estimated that archaeology has uncovered no more than 2% of what needs to be uncovered. And what has been uncovered consistently adds to the evidence that our Bible today is reliable and is the product of what the original writers penned during the days of both the Old and New Testaments.

Now having explored both the manuscripts and archaeology, let's consider a third, and perhaps the greatest evidence for the trustworthiness of Scripture. I'm referring to the unique quality of the Bible, compared to all other religions – prophecy.

Prophecy – The Master Key

Out of all the types of evidence to support the validity of Scripture, I believe that prophecy is the *"Master Key"* that unlocks the most compelling evidence. Why do I say that? Because no other religious or *"holy"* book is prophetic. Muhammad did not make prophetic statements so that you could look at history and say, *"He prophesied this event and it came true, based on historical fact"*. Buddha did not predict future events. But Jesus predicted future events that you can trace to historical fulfillment and so did the prophets and apostles do the same. In fact, 25% of the Bible was prophetic when written. There are approximately 2,500 prophecies in the Bible, 2,000 of which have been fulfilled, while another 500 have yet to be fulfilled, but will be in the future.

In the Old Testament, there are over 1,800 references to the return of Christ, as well as many that focused on His first coming to the earth, such as where He would be born (Micah 5:2); where He would minister (Isaiah 9:1-2); that He would be born of a virgin (Isaiah 7:14); that He would be put to death and buried in a rich man's tomb (Isaiah 53); that He would be raised from the dead (Psalm 16:10), as well as many other prophetic statements. In fact, if I read Psalm 22:1 to a group of people, I believe the majority would conclude that I was reading from one of the Gospels. I know because I've read that passage during communion services and then told people from where it came and I could see the astonished faces staring back at me. Try it yourself by reading that passage to a friend who knows something about the Bible and then ask, *"From which Gospel do you think I'm reading?"*, or you might ask, *"From what passage of Scripture do you think I'm reading?"* When you inform them that what you were reading was written 1,000 years before the birth of Christ, it makes an impression on people concerning the unity and accuracy of the Bible.

I'd like you to consider one more issue about prophecy. Every prophecy concerning Jesus' first coming to earth was fulfilled literally and in exact detail. He wasn't born in a place that looked like Bethlehem or that had a similar name. Micah said that Messiah would be born in Bethlehem, and so when the wise men came to honor the new *"King of the Jews"*, they asked King Herod, *"Where is the one who has been born king of the Jews?"* (Matthew 2:2) Astonished at the request of these visitors from the East, King Herod called the chief priests and teachers of the Law. They responded by quoting from the prophet Micah – *"But you, Bethlehem, in the land of Judah, are by no means least among the rulers of Judah; for out of you will come a ruler who will be the shepherd of my people Israel"* (Matthew 2:6) And where did the wise men go from there? To the city located about five miles south of Jerusalem – Bethlehem.

Now if the prophecies concerning Jesus' first arrival on earth were fulfilled literally and in detail, how do you think prophecies not yet fulfilled will occur? Would it not seem feasible that they also will be fulfilled literally and in exact detail? If that is the case, we should know what God tells us about the future and then align our personal lives accordingly. Let's consider a few unfulfilled prophecies that still await their fulfillment.

Jesus told His disciples that He would return and take them to be with Him in the future – *"In my Father's house are many rooms; if it were not so, I would have told you. I am going there to prepare a place for you. And if I go and prepare a place for you I will come back and take you to be with me that you also may be where I am"* (John 14:2-4).

The Apostle Paul builds on this prophecy when he writes, *"Listen, I tell you a mystery: We will not all sleep, but we will all be changed – in a flash, in the twinkling of an eye, at the last trumpet. For the trumpet will sound, the dead will be raised imperishable, and we will be changed"* (1 Corinthians 15:51-52). And then the Apostle writes a similar prophecy to the believers in Thessalonica by predicting, *"For the Lord himself will come down from heaven, with a loud command, with the voice of the archangel and with the trumpet call of God, and the dead in Christ will rise first. After that, we who are still alive and are left will be caught up together with them in the clouds to meet the Lord in the air. And so we will be with the Lord forever"* (1 Thessalonians 4:16-17).

Is there any reason to believe that those prophecies will not actually take place? Is there any reason to believe that though God fulfilled every prophecy concerning the first coming of Christ in a literal and detailed way, that He would now change how prophecy will be fulfilled? That's another one of those decisions you'll have to make for yourself. I'm just raising the question so that you challenge your assumptions and do your own research.

Manuscripts, archaeology and prophecy are excellent witnesses to the validity of Scripture, but let's add a few more like-minded witnesses, like the survival of Scripture over the centuries against dictators and countries that ban it, burn it and forbid even reading it, the character of the authors, internal evidence, the testimony of others and changed lives, and the testimony of Jesus Christ Himself. We'll begin with the survival of the Bible from destruction and criticism.

Survival

No other book in the history of mankind has been so maligned, hated, ridiculed and banned as has the Bible. There must be something inside to attract so much hatred. What could it be? Is it possible that it speaks about sin and God's judgment of sin? Could it be that it sets standards and moral values far above man's comfort zone? Is it possible that if people truly believe the Bible, they may want a different society than the one in which they live and tolerate? All these reasons are possible causes for man's ridicule and hatred of the Bible.

But every attempt to destroy or bury the Bible from man's conscience may be victorious for a short time, but eventually it keeps rising from the dead. I appreciate the way Dr. Bernard Ramm put it when he wrote, ***"A thousand times over, the death knell of the Bible has been sounded, the funeral procession formed, the inscription cut on the tombstone, and committal read. But somehow the corpse never stays put"***.[1]

1. Josh McDowell, *The New Evidence That Demands A Verdict* (Nashville, TN: Thomas Nelson Publishers. P.11.)

The Character Of The Authors

One of the first things I do when I see a new title of a book is to read about the author. What are the author's credentials? In other words, *"Does he know what his talking about?" "Do others support his character or scholarship?" "Does he have an ax to grind?" "Can I trust that what he is writing is actually true?"* These same questions can be applied to the writers of the Scriptures.

What were the Scripture writers like? Did they know what they were talking about? Did what they said actually happen the way they said it happened? Normally, a man like Moses would write about his great victory of bringing the people of Israel out of Egypt. And you would expect David to write about all of his exploits in conquering other people groups and his victories on the battlefield. And someone like Matthew and John would probably want to do a lot of name-dropping. After all, they lived with Jesus for three years and saw His miracles, heard all of His sermons, and enjoyed listening to Him put the religious leaders in their place. And then there is the Apostle Paul. If he were to write anything, he would probably spend most of his time informing people of how he was able to climb the ladder of Judaism, beginning as an apprentice to Gamalio.

However, one of the unique qualities of the Bible is that it tells it like it is. If this were a book written merely by men and they are speaking about personal experiences, you'd expect them to somehow show themselves in the best light. They probably wouldn't be talking about their failures, doubts, or sins. And yet, the Bible holds nothing back. Moses wrote about his act of murder. David wrote about his adultery. Matthew and John wrote about their own lack of faith. And then there was the Apostle Paul. Are his Epistles filled with bragging rights? Judge for yourself. He wrote to young Timothy, *"Here is a trustworthy saying that deserves full* acceptance: *Christ Jesus came into the world to save sinners – of whom I am the worst*" (1 Timothy 1:15).

And what about their qualifications? Well, if we were looking for mostly highly educated men with PhDs, we'd be sorely disappointed with these writers. But consider who these writers really were. They were men who lived lives that they did not choose and accomplished tasks for which they never would have volunteered. Furthermore, they were men whose lives changed drastically after they met Jesus or when they had an encounter with God. With men like these, you have the type of author who will speak truth. All of the men mentioned above either had an encounter with God, like Moses and the burning bush, or had been with or at least had seen Jesus. And because of those encounters, they had something to say.

The Internal Evidence Of Scripture – The Bible's Own Testimony

What does the Bible have to say for itself? First, it claims that it contains the very words of God and not man. When the Apostle Paul raises the question whether there is an advantage of being a Jew, he replies, *"First of all, they have been entrusted with the very words of God"* (Romans 3:2). The Bible is not merely about God, but it also contains the *"very words of God"*. In fact, those words are *"God-breathed"* words (2 Timothy 3:16).

The phrase *"God-breathed"* is also translated *"inspired"*. The writings were inspired, not the writers. They were just men writing in obedience and prompted by the Holy Spirit. What do I mean by *"prompted by the Spirit?"* When the writers penned those words, they did not do so on their own. The Apostle Peter informs us **"For prophecy never had its origin in the will of man, but men**

spoke from God as they were carried along by the Holy Spirit" (2 Peter 1:21). The phrase *"carried along"* is a Greek word used of the wind blowing the sails of a ship to move it across the waters. The Spirit of God *"moved"* them to write what they wrote. None of the men ever dreamed that God would choose to use them to write words that would last thousands of years after they put down their pens. Little could they have imagined that what they wrote changed the course of history.

When the Apostle Paul wrote to the believers in Thessalonica, he commended them by saying, *"And we also thank God continually because, when you received the word of God, which you heard from us, you accepted it not as the word of men, but as it actually is, the word of God, which is at work in you who believe"* (1 Thessalonians 2:13).

Furthermore, throughout the Old Testament, the phrase, *"Thus says the Lord"* is found 415 times. The phrase, *"God said"* is found 52 times. And *"The Lord Said"* is found 275 times. In other words, God is speaking so man can record what was on His mind and heart 742 times in the Scriptures.

The Testimony Of Others

What have others said about the Bible? Listen to some people whom you have some familiarity:

President George Washington – *"It is impossible to govern a nation without God or the Bible"* (bibleornot.org)

President John Quincy Adams – *"So great is my veneration for the Bible that the earlier my children begin to read it the more confident will be my hope that they will prove useful citizens* of their country and respectable members of society." *(ministers. bestfriend.com)*

President Abraham Lincoln - *"I believe the Bible is the best gift God has ever given to man. All the good from The Savior of the world is communicated to us through this Book."* (goodreads.com)

Chief Justice John Jay, the first Chief-Justice of the Supreme Court – *"The Bible is the best of all books, for it is the word of God and teaches us the way to be happy in this world and in the next. Continue therefore to read it and to regulate your life by its precepts."* (usa.church) (U.S. History Quotes About God And The Bible)

Daniel Webster – *"If there is anything in my thoughts or style to commend, the credit is due to my parents for instilling in me an early love of the Scriptures. If we abide by the principles taught in the Bible, our country will go on prospering and to prosper; but if we and our posterity neglect its instructions and authority, no man can tell how sudden a catastrophe may overwhelm us and bury all our glory in profound obscurity."*
(Bible Quotes From Famous People http://www.turnback togod.com/bible-quotes-from-famous people/#ixzz4Gagx9Y9P)

President Harry S. Truman - *"The fundamental basis of this nation's law was given to Moses on the Mount. The fundamental basis of our Bill of Rights comes from the teaching we get from Exodus and St. Matthew, from Isaiah and St. Paul. I don't think we emphasize that enough these days. If we don't have the proper fundamental moral background, we will finally end up with a totalitarian government which does not believe in the right for anybody except the state."*
Bible Quotes From Famous People http://www.turnback togod.com/bible-quotes-from-famous-people/#ixzz4GahwGFv5

President Ronald Reagan - *"Within the covers of the Bible are the answers for all the problems men face."* (goodreads.com)

Jesus Christ - *"This is what I told you while I was still with you: Everything must be fulfilled that is written about me in the Law of Moses, the Prophets, and the Psalms"* (Luke 24:44). The Lord was referring to the Old Testament, since the New Testament had not yet been written. He is saying that He can be found in the Old Testament. The three divisions of the Hebrew Bible (The Law, The Prophets, and the Writings) all speak about Him. Therefore, you should be able to find Jesus throughout the Old Testament and we do.

"I tell you the truth, until heaven and earth disappear, not the smallest letter, not the least stroke of a pen, will by any means disappear from the Law until everything is accomplished" (Matthew 5:18).

"Heaven and earth will pass away, but my words will never pass away." (Luke 21:33)

So now we've looked at evidence on various levels to determine just how trustworthy the Bible is. We checked out manuscripts, archaeology, prophecy, survival, the character of the writers, the internal evidence of Scripture and the testimony of others. But let's consider one more piece of evidence for the validity of Scripture.

Changed lives – does it work?

It's often been said that the proof is in the pudding. In other words, how do you know that pudding is good if you don't taste it? Likewise, how do you know that the Bible is true and will make a difference in your life if you don't read it and put it to work?

Therefore, let's consider some individuals whose lives were dramatically changed for the good of others because of the Bible.

Rather than list individuals whose lives have been changed by reading or studying the Bible, I want to share with you what the Bible claims it can do for a person.

Claim #1 – **It can lead a person to eternal life** – *"But these are written that you may believe that Jesus is the Christ, the son of God, and that by believing you may have life in his name"* (John 20:31). The Bible is the tool God uses to bring conviction into our hearts and the desire to turn from our sin to Jesus Christ. The Apostle Paul emphasizes this truth when he writes, *"Consequently, faith comes from hearing the message, and the message is heard through the word of Christ"* (Romans 10:9-10).

Claim #2 - **It can change a person from despair to hope** – *"For everything that was written in the past was written to teach us, so that through endurance and the encouragement of the Scriptures we might have hope"* (Romans 15:4).

Claim #3 – **It can make a person wiser than someone older and more experienced than he** – *"I have more insight than all my teachers, for I meditate on your statutes. I have more understanding than the elders, for I obey your precepts"* (Psalm 119:99-100).

Claim #4 – **It can protect a person from falling into sin and rebellion** – *"How can a young man keep his way pure? By living according to your word"* (Psalm 119:9).

Claim #5 – **It can protect us from placing too much confidence in that which most people greatly admire:**

- **Pleasure** – *"I denied myself nothing my eyes desired; I refused my heart no pleasure. My heart took delight in all my work, and this was the reward for all my labor. Yet when I surveyed all that my hands had done and what I had toiled to achieve, everything was meaningless, a chasing after the wind; nothing was gained under the sun"* (Ecclesiastes 2:10-11).

- **Fortune** – *"Whoever loves money never has money enough; whoever loves wealth is never satisfied with his income. This too is meaningless"* (Ecclesiastes 5:10). *"Be sure to know the condition of your flocks, give careful attention to your herds; for riches do not endure forever, and a crown is not secure for all generations"* (Proverbs 27:23-24).

- **Power** – *"He changes times and seasons; he sets up kings and deposes them"* (Daniel 2:21).

- **Beauty** – *"Charm is deceptive, and beauty is fleeting: but a woman who fears the Lord is to be praised"* (Proverbs 31:30).

- **Plans** for the Future – *"Now listen, you who say, 'Today or tomorrow we will go to this or that city, spend a year there, carry on business and make money.' Why, you do not even know what will happen tomorrow. What is your life? You ae a mist that appears for a time and then vanishes. Instead, you ought to say, 'If it is the Lord's will we will live and do this or that'"* (James 4:13-15). *"When their spirit departs, they return to the ground; on that very day their plans come to nothing"* (Psalms 146:4).

As I close out this chapter, I'd like to share with you how the Bible has changed my own life. I was never much of a student in school. In fact, I was more of the class clown than anything else. Many of my teachers did not think I would ever get into college, let alone do something worthwhile. In fact, my homeroom teacher told me on one occasion in front of the class, *"Yohn, you'll never amount to anything"*. He was obviously provoked at me because he knew I wasn't paying any attention to him as he lectured. And, without a change in my attitude, he was exactly right.

I did graduate from high school (barely) and entered a local college on academic probation, and after my first year, I was still on academic probation. And then God captured my heart and gave me a desire to know and study the Scriptures. That fall I entered Philadelphia College of Bible and began a spiritual and mental transformation, as I became more and more exposed to the Scriptures. And from college I moved on to seminary, where I met a Professor named Howard G. Hendricks, better known by his students as *"Prof"* and his friends as *"Howie"*. Once again another transformation took place, for Prof Hendricks taught me how to study the Bible for myself, and I have never stopped that process.

With three years of Hebrew, six and a half years of Greek, plus a Masters and Doctoral Degree, the Lord opened doors I had never expected to be open, such as becoming the Dean of Biblical and Theological Studies at a University, developing two Masters Programs for the school, writing curriculum and books, and now teaching as an Adjunct Faculty Member. Today I am far different than that high school student who was told by his homeroom teacher, *"Yohn, you'll never amount to anything"*. The process moving from the past to the present is known as God's unlimited grace.

You may never study the Bible on a professional level, but I guarantee that when you take the Scriptures seriously and commit yourself to read and study God's Word, you too will experience a gradual and daily transformation within. And that is when others will notice that there is something different in your attitude and lifestyle. Some will be thrilled at the changes taking place, while others may shun you because you are not the person that you used to be.

15

Love that Demands a Response

Before we look at how we might respond to God's love, let's review the many ways in which God has demonstrated His love to us. It began with, *"In the beginning God created. . ."*. Like the parents who want to provide the best for one of their greatest achievements in life, bringing new life into the world, so did our Creator want a special, perfect place where His creation of mankind would have an environment that would never again be duplicated. God's ultimate creation would have a beautiful surrounding, a never-ending supply of food and water, the perfect work environment, and a family to love and nurture in the ways of the Lord. And when mankind failed to obey the Lord's one negative command, sin and death entered the world. But out of His love for mankind, God provided a covering for their sin and a way back to Him.

However, mankind became increasingly evil in the sight of God and so the Lord determined to bring an end to His special creation except for one man and his family. Once again motivated by love, God provided for man's sin by directing Noah to build a craft large enough for Noah, his family, and the animals of God's choice.

And yet, after the great flood, mankind spurned God's love by building a tower to remain where he was and disobey God's directive to populate the earth. Secondly, mankind decided to establish his own worship by building a tower to the heavens, and repudiated God's approach to worship. So, God confused mankind's language and man scattered across the earth.

Once again, God wanted to get His love story out to the peoples across the earth, so He chose one man, who would be the father of one family, and eventually one nation, and finally many nations. Through Abraham God was going to communicate His love and in the distant future, provide the greatest love-gift ever given, named Jesus Christ.

As one of Abraham's people groups began to grow while living in Egypt, they were subjected to slave labor for 430 years. As they cried out to their God, He demonstrated His love for them by raising up a shepherd from Midian, who once was a Prince in Egypt. His name was Moses. Because of God's great love for His people, The Lord delivered this people group from Egyptian bondage and provided for them over a forty-year period as they trekked through the desert. After the first generation died, due to unbelief, God brought the second generation, plus Joshua and Caleb, (from the first generation) into the Land which He had promised Abraham.

This people group eventually became the nation of Israel, who rebelled time after time against the God who loved them again and again. So, God had to deal with the people's sins through removing the Northern Kingdom of Israel by the Assyrians and the Southern Kingdom of Judah by the Babylonians. But God was not finished with the nation He chose to represent Him on earth. He brought back the people of Judah and resettled them in the Land we call Israel. They once again built a Temple that was enlarged by King Herod. Though they had a Temple, they were no longer a sovereign nation. When God's greatest demonstration of love came in the Person of His Son, Jesus Christ, the nation rejected Him as their Messiah and the Romans crucified Him.

We might think that after such a rejection, God was finished with the nation of Israel forever. However, He never stopped loving those He chose, but put them aside for a time and raised up another people group, which later became known as the Church. Once again God was in the business of spreading His love to the nations of the world, and the Church is now carrying that message to the nations of the world. And what about Israel? Has God discarded her forever, or replaced her with the Church? Not according to the Apostle Paul who raised two questions concerning God's relationship with this nation. He first asked, *"I ask then, has God rejected his people? By no means! For I myself am an Israelite, a descendant of Abraham, a member of the tribe of Benjamin"* (Romans 11:1).

Later in his letter to the Roman believers, Paul raises another question, *"So I ask, did they stumble in order that they may fall? By no means! Rather through their trespass salvation has come to the Gentiles, so as to make Israel jealous."* (Romans 11:11).

As I've studied the Scriptures over a 50 plus year period, I've concluded that God is not finished with Israel. I believe He has put her to the side *"until the fullness of the Gentiles"* (Luke 21:24). In other words, Gentile rule over Israel must come to an end. Many believe that this occurred in 1948. If that is true, then the rest of this prophecy awaits future fulfillment of the "New Covenant" (Jeremiah 31:31), when God puts His Spirit into the hearts of the people of Israel (Ezekiel 36:26).

I believe the first part of this Covenant has been fulfilled for Israel. He said, *"For I will take you out of the nations; I will gather you from all the countries and bring you back into your own land*" (Ezekiel 34:24). This would not be speaking of their captivity in Babylon because that was only one nation and God said that He would bring them out of the "**nations**" and gather them from "**all the countries**". When Israel returned from Babylon under Zerubbabel, then Ezra and later Nehemiah, they returned from one country, Babylon.

Therefore, I believe that this return to the Land part of the passage has been fulfilled. Ever since 586 B.C., Israel was no longer a sovereign nation, even when it returned from Babylon. But after WWII, God began to bring them back from the nations of the world and in 1948 they officially became a sovereign nation once again. But immediately after that declaration of Independence, five surrounding Arab nations determined to wipe Israel from the face of the earth: Egypt, Jordan, Syria, Lebanon and Iraq. And yet, God once again spared His people from annihilation, as Israel not only defeated the five nations, but gained even more territory than they previously possessed.

However, Israel is in the Land in unbelief, awaiting that great day when God will give them a new heart and will place His Spirit into them, so they might turn back to Him and recognize the Messiah they have rejected for over 2,000 years.

But in the meantime, God is spreading His love world-wide through His Church, made up of both Jew and Gentile. By the Church, I am not referring to either a building nor a denomination. The Church is made up of individual believers world-wide. The Bible refers to these believers as "saints", who have been "set apart" from the worldview that excludes God, and have been brought into a body of believers, who have received God's love by receiving His Son, Jesus Christ into their lives.

God's love is universal and it is national, but also very personal. The Apostle Paul's prayer for individual believers, wherever we live, is this – *"And I pray that you, being rooted and established in love, may have power, together with all the saints, to grasp how wide and long and high and deep is the love of Christ. . ."* (Ephesians 3:17-18).

But is it possible to ever lose the love of God? Not at all. Paul also writes, *"For I am convinced that neither death nor life, neither angels nor demons, neither the present nor the future, nor any powers, neither height nor depth, nor anything else in all creation, will be able to separate us from the love of God that is in Christ Jesus our Lord"* (Romans 8:37-19).

In conclusion, we've discovered that the Bible is not a mere collection of sixty-six independent books. Rather, these Scriptures reveal the love God has for mankind in general and each one of us. It's an agape love, one that never fails and yet was very costly for the Lover. And it's a love that demands a response.

God's love is too great to be ignored. And it would be foolish to reject. Therefore, if you have never asked Christ into your life, I would encourage you to respond by receiving God's love through His greatest love gift, His Son Jesus Christ. He wants you to not only know He loves you, but also greatly desires that you receive that love, and as a bonus, eternal life.

Listen to the words of the Apostle John when he states, *"He came to that which was his own, but his own did not receive him. **Yet to all who received him,** to those who believed in his name, he gave the right to become children of God – children born not of natural descent, nor of human decision or a husband's will, but born of God."* (John 1:12-13)

Can you think of any reason why you shouldn't enjoy God's love gift? If not, why not receive His greatest love gift ever given, His Son Jesus Christ? That love gift will never grow old and you'll never out-live it. It is eternal and so are you.

If you have received this love gift, the next step you'll want to take is to share it with others. People in your family, in the workplace, and at school are looking for love. One that will give them hope, a second chance, or a new beginning. They need to hear about the One who alone can provide that love and you are in the position to share it with those in your world of influence. Why not make today that new beginning for yourself?

CPSIA information can be obtained
at www.ICGtesting.com
Printed in the USA
LVOW03s0022100318
569341LV00003B/5/P